Thackeray at Work

Thackeray at Work

J. A. SUTHERLAND

UNIVERSITY OF LONDON
THE ATHLONE PRESS
1974

Published by
THE ATHLONE PRESS
UNIVERSITY OF LONDON
at 4 *Gower Street, London* WC1

Distributed by
Tiptree Book Services Ltd
Tiptree, Essex

U.S.A. and Canada
Humanities Press Inc
New York

ISBN 0 485 11146 2

Printed in Great Britain by
WESTERN PRINTING SERVICES LTD
BRISTOL

Preface

This study depends very largely on unpublished manuscript materials and my gratitude is due to the following libraries, librarians and individuals who have allowed me access and permission: Mr Robert H. Taylor and the University Library at Princeton, the Pierpont Morgan Library, the New York Public Library Manuscripts Division, the College Library at Harvard, the Beinecke Rare Books and Manuscripts Library at Yale, the British Museum Manuscripts Department, Trinity College Library, Cambridge, the Headmaster and Librarian of Charterhouse School.

Some parts of this book have appeared before in print. The second part of the chapter on *Vanity Fair* ('The Waterloo Number') was published in the *Princeton University Library Chronicle*, 1972; the third part of the same chapter ('The "Vanity Fair" Interpolations') appeared in the *Journal of Narrative Technique*, 1973; and the fourth part ('Time and the Novel') first appeared in *Anglia*, 1971. The chapter '*Henry Esmond* and the Virtues of Carelessness' first appeared in *Modern Philology* (the University of Chicago Press), 1971. I am grateful to the editors and publishers for permission to reprint. I have taken the opportunity to correct some errors of fact or emphasis in revising these pieces for this study.

I have had the benefit of scholarly assistance from a number of sources and I particularly want to thank Professor K. J. Fielding of Edinburgh University for his untiring and expert help over many years. I also owe a particular debt of gratitude to Professor Kathleen Tillotson, who pointed out to me an egregious error in my account of the plans Thackeray made for the Waterloo Number of *Vanity Fair*. At every step in this study I have been assisted by the critical, biographical and editorial work of Gordon N. Ray, an assistance which I gratefully acknowledge. I should like to thank Dr Ray and Mrs Belinda Norman-Butler for permission to quote from Thackeray's *Letters and Private Papers*.

J.A.S.

Contents

Illustrations

Note on Symbols used in the Text

Crossings out in Thackeray's manuscripts are indicated thus:
| THE ESTATE OF CASTLEWOOD |

Interlineations are indicated thus:
⟨the estate of Castlewood⟩

In general only those manuscript variations or alterations which are significant to the argument have been transcribed. I have regularised some of Thackeray's habitual abbreviations and, in places, added the inverted commas which he left to the printer.

Introduction

When we congratulated him, many years ago, on the touch in Vanity Fair in which Becky *admires* her husband when he is giving Lord Steyne the chastisement which ruins *her* for life, 'Well', he said, 'when I wrote the sentence, I slapped my fist on the table, and said *that* is a touch of genius.'[1]

'In authorship', wrote George Eliot, 'I hold carelessness to be a mortal sin.'[2] By this stern law Thackeray would seem to be damned. Of all the great Victorian novelists he is the most casual and, apparently, the most inattentive to his art. He would, he optimistically said, write 'careful books' after he had made his £10,000 a year[3]—which was another way of saying next year, sometime, never.

Thackeray's contemporary and later admirers have never been entirely easy on this subject. Charlotte Brontë complained outright about his 'criminal carelessness of great faculties',[4] and even in the generosity of an obituary tribute Dickens could not refrain from declaring with an oddly Pecksniffian turn of phrase: 'I thought [Thackeray] too much feigned a want of earnestness, and that he made a pretence of undervaluing his art, which was not good for the art that he held in trust.'[5] Dickens's *feigned* gives Thackeray some benefit of doubt. Less kind critics must have found that a verbal sketch provided by Eyre Crowe in *Thackeray's Haunts and Homes* captured their notion of the novelist *working* as he lay on his bed 'dictating *Esmond* all day, while whiffing his cigar'.[6] How such a dilettante could on occasion turn out great fiction was no mystery to A. A. Jack—Thackeray was simply luckier than other lazy men:

His manner of writing was desultory, and he was always ready to give rein to whatever mood was uppermost. He rarely formed any conception of a book before he had finished it, and never took the trouble to think about the canons of his art. He stumbled on right methods, just as he floundered into mistakes.[7]

(One may pause to wish that all careless novelists would 'stumble' on an *Esmond*.) Jack is not so weighty a critic that one need accept his unsupported assertion. But we have it on the reliable, first-hand testimony of J. T. Fields, a sympathetic and intimate friend of Thackeray in later life, that the novelist's motto was indeed 'Avoid performing today, if possible, what can be postponed till to-morrow'[8]—be unprepared, in other words. And according to Whibley, the sternest but by no means the stupidest of commentators, Thackeray 'permitted most of his books to write themselves'.[9]

One could multiply similar examples from first readers down to the latest critical studies. But I want to select from the chorus of opinion on this subject what I take to be the strongest and most persuasive voice, that of Anthony Trollope. Trollope wrote a critical biography of Thackeray in 1879 for the 'English Men of Letters' series. In it he delivered his considered opinion of Thackeray the craftsman: 'unsteadfast, idle, changeable of purpose . . . no man ever failed more generally than he to put his best foot foremost' (19).[10] He laid the blame squarely on 'that propensity to wandering which came to Thackeray because of his idleness . . . Though he can settle himself down to his pen and ink,—not always even to that without a struggle, but to that with sufficient burst of energy to produce a large average amount of work,—he cannot settle himself down to the task of contriving a story' (137–8). This was written fifteen years after Thackeray's death in that period when, inevitably, a great author's reputation must pass through a posthumous trough. But the date alone does not explain why Trollope, of all people, should have delivered himself of so harsh a judgement nor why he should have repeated it so often and so vehemently.[11] It cannot be charged to ignorance—Trollope knew Thackeray as a close friend; neither can it be charged to malice —Trollope idolised Thackeray and only uncomfortable honesty drove him to utter an attack which would pain his friend's surviving family; least of all can it be charged to professional antipathy—Trollope, the 'lesser Thackeray', was a self-confessed disciple.

It should be emphasised that what one is thinking of here is not the trivial error in detail or oversight which an artist working at full stretch can hardly help committing. When *Notes and Queries* came out in 1854 its contributors, more sprightly than today's scholars but just as punctilious, had fine sport quizzing Thackeray's fiction; in his then emerging novel, *The Newcomes*, there were found no less than fifty 'mistakes' and one querist wound up by asking outright 'surely no author has a right to treat his readers with such carelessness?'[12] To which one answers—yes, he does have this right. Probably all novelists and particularly serialists pulsing out 15,000 words a month perpetrate the kind of mistake *Notes and Queries* lists: inconsistent Christian names, a little bad grammar, occasionally slipshod chronology. Even that perfectionist among plot-wrights, Wilkie Collins, got the time-scheme of the *Woman in White* slightly wrong in its first serialised version. Such carelessness, Thackeray would counter (and we should agree), is no mortal sin but venial and can surely be forgiven:

I pray gentle readers to deal kindly with their humble servant's manifold shortcomings, blunders, and slips of memory. As sure as I read a page of my own composition, I find a fault or two, half-a-dozen. Jones is called Brown. Brown, who is dead, is brought to life. Aghast, and months after the number was printed, I saw that

I had called Philip Firmin, Clive Newcome. Now Clive Newcome is the hero of another story by the reader's most obedient writer. The two men are as different, in my mind's eye, as—as Lord Palmerston and Mr. Disraeli let us say. But there is that blunder at page 990, line 76, volume 84 of the *Cornhill Magazine*, and it is past mending; and I wish in my life I had made no worse blunders or errors than that which is hereby acknowledged. (xvii, 593)[13]

As he cheerfully admits, names, numbers and time-schemes were notoriously hazardous for Thackeray. Few readers will have failed to catch him out somewhere and his lapses are famous enough for a tolerant Saintsbury to call them in his definitive 'Oxford Edition', Thackeray's 'sign-manual' (xvii, 345).[14] No-one other than a pedant need have his pleasure in reading *Esmond* or his estimate of the novelist diminished by the fact that Frank Castlewood is on occasion called Arthur, that Beatrix quotes from a book some forty years before it was written or that Rachel Esmond is given two impossibly separate dates of death in the same novel.[15]

But the gravamen of Trollope's charge is much more serious than this and is not to be shrugged off as a mere side-effect of serialisation. Thackeray's 'carelessness' he observes, is not simply a matter of haste—most of the great Victorian novelists had to write more rapidly than they would have liked to—but of concentration. Trollope's objection may be summed up in his maxim that 'to think of a story is much harder work than to write it' (123). Thackeray, allegedly, failed to 'think' in this way and Trollope detects in his fiction a pervasive 'touch of vagueness which indicates that his pen was not firm while he was using it' (19).

I will permit myself a longish example to show how this 'touch of vagueness' can actually appear on the printed page. The following passage is taken from the narrative of the printed and revised *Esmond*, a novel which, it will be recalled, was *not*

4

written under the 'life and death'[16] pressure of serialisation. It comes at the climax of Harry's plot to restore the Stuarts to the English throne. The Old Pretender has been smuggled to Kensington disguised as Frank Castlewood's secretary, Monsieur Baptiste. Once arrived he has changed places with Castlewood, though the reason for the change is inscrutable. The servants have been deceived in advance by a portrait of the Pretender which is displayed in the Castlewoods' town house as one of the long-absent Frank. It is not the easiest of passages to follow but I would ask the reader to spend a minute or two examining Thackeray's description of the success of this operation and the part played by Lockwood, Esmond's manservant:

Esmond's man, honest John Lockwood, had served his master and the family all his life, and the colonel knew that he could answer for John's fidelity as for his own. John returned with the horses from Rochester betimes the next morning, and the colonel gave him to understand that on going to Kensington, where he was free of the servants' hall, and indeed courting Mrs. Beatrix's maid, he was to ask no questions, and betray no surprise, but to vouch stoutly that the young gentleman he should see in a red coat there was my Lord Viscount Castlewood, and that his attendant in grey was Monsieur Baptiste the Frenchman. He was to tell his friends in the kitchen such stories as he remembered of my lord viscount's youth at Castlewood; what a wild boy he was; how he used to drill Jack and cane him, before ever he was a soldier; everything, in fine, he knew respecting my lord viscount's early days. Jack's ideas of painting had not been much cultivated during his residence in Flanders with his master; and, before my young lord's return, he had been easily got to believe that the picture brought over from Paris, and now hanging in Lady Castlewood's drawing-room, was a perfect likeness of her son, the young lord. And the domestics, having all seen the picture many times, and catching but a momentary, imperfect glimpse of the two strangers on the night of their arrival, never had a reason

5

to doubt the fidelity of the portrait; and next day, when they saw the original of the piece habited exactly as he was represented in the painting, with the same periwig, ribbons, and uniform of the Guard, quite naturally addressed the gentleman as my Lord Castlewood, my lady viscountess's son. (416–17)

There was, incidentally, no break in composition to account for the fact that Lockwood in the first part of the paragraph— and in the rest of the chapter—is a knowing accomplice in the conspiracy and in the second part of the paragraph an unknowing dupe 'easily got to believe that the picture brought over from Paris, and now hanging in Lady Castlewood's drawing-room, was a perfect likeness of her son, the young lord'. One can, however, hazard a guess at how this oddity came about. Elsewhere in the novel Thackeray is characteristically liberal in bestowing Christian names on Lockwood, who has served Esmond since his youth. He is variously John, Job, Jack and Tom. One assumes that here the novelist absent-mindedly takes John and Jack Lockwood to be different people, the one ignorant, the other enlightened about the goings-on at Kensington.

Similar cases can be found in all the major novels.[17] It would be unfair to claim that they are at all numerous but there are enough to make us suspicious and more attentive to Trollope when he asserts that Thackeray did not sufficiently 'think' about his story. And if we register these lapses the effect is peculiarly destructive of fictional illusion. In the last section of *Esmond* it is vital for suspense and pace that clarity be maintained. Such inefficiencies as the above trip the reader when it is necessary that he should be carried away in the narrative. There is an area of haziness around John-Jack Lockwood, an important agent in the restoration plot (itself none too clear), which smudges the novel's climactic episode. The pen, as Trollope would say, has not been held firmly.

II

Modern critics and readers who appreciate Thackeray tend simply to bypass without trying to answer what we may call the Trollopian objection. Yet it still hangs over the novelist and is still invoked by those critics, the majority one suspects, who do not appreciate Thackeray. The uncompromising force of Trollope's 'It was his nature to be idle' (15) can often be felt bolstering more subtle objections that Thackeray has no 'daemon' or is not really 'serious' or is a 'novelist *manqué*'.[18]

The following study may be seen as an attempt to answer Trollope. But 'answer' does not necessarily imply 'refutation': I would not deny, for instance, that there is a culpable deal of 'idleness' and 'carelessness' in the composition of Thackeray's fiction. These, however, I would take in the forgiving spirit that Henry James takes George Eliot's formlessness: 'the greatest minds have the defects of their qualities.'[19] Thackeray's qualities are intimately linked with the immediacy and opportunism of his writing methods. He is, one would guess, of all Victorian novelists the one who throve best in the bustle of monthly serialisation—not because he was capable of foreseeing all the future plot and character developments of his story but because he was gifted with a wonderfully reliable inventiveness. The instinctive way in which he wrote and the kind of success he achieved is described in one of the late *Roundabout Papers*:

Alexandre Dumas describes himself, when inventing the plan of a work, as lying silent on his back for two whole days on the deck of a yacht in a Mediterranean port. At the end of the two days he arose, and called for dinner. In those two days he had built his plot. He had moulded a mighty clay, to be cast presently in perennial brass. The chapters, the characters, the incidents, the combinations, were all arranged in the artist's brain ere he set a pen to paper. My Pegasus won't fly, so as to let me survey the field below me. He has no wings, he is blind of one eye certainly, he is restive, stubborn, slow; crops a hedge when he ought to be galloping, or gallops when he ought to be quiet. He never will show off when I want him. Sometimes he goes at a pace which surprises me. Sometimes, when I most wish him to make the running, the brute turns restive, and I am obliged to let him take his own time. I wonder do other novel-writers experience this fatalism? They *must* go a certain way, in spite of themselves. I have been surprised at the observations made by some of my characters. It seems as if an occult power was moving the pen. The personage does or says something, and I ask, how the Dickens did he come to think of that? Every man has remarked in dreams, the vast dramatic power which is sometimes evinced; I won't say the surprising power, for nothing does surprise you in dreams. But those strange characters you meet make instant observations of which you never can have thought previously. In like manner, the imagination foretells things. (xvii, 596–7)

Writing as he did one can see how Thackeray's 'touches of genius' and his 'touches of vagueness' might stem from the same root. He was, above all, a spontaneously creative artist. Often, of course, he had to be: few novelists can have produced so much of their *oeuvre* with the printer's devil waiting in the hall and publishers complaining that he was 'dreadfully unpunctual'.[20] First thoughts, corrected version and fair copy were not unusually pressed into one act of the pen by Thackeray. Frequently he presented to his friends the spectacle of a man worried literally to death by deadlines. 'I can conceive nothing more harassing in the literary way than [Thackeray's] way of living from hand to mouth. I mean in regard to the way in which he furnishes food for the printer's devil':[21] so J. L. Motley lamented on seeing the novelist labour against the clock in the British Museum. But one need not commiserate with Motley about Thackeray's 'hand to mouth' method of work. He was by nature what the harassment of serialisation forced him to be, a one-draft writer. Even at the prosperous end of his life, when he could take his time, he remained essentially what he had been in his youth and poverty. Leslie Stephen, who married one of Thackeray's daughters, writes in a letter to an American bibliographer about the manuscript of the *Roundabout Papers*:

... in later life he seems to have written slowly but definitively. There is a MS. of 'Esmond' now in Trinity College Library at Cambridge, of which about half was dictated. 'Esmond' is certainly one of his most finished works in point of style and it is therefore remarkable, I think, that the final form seems to have been given at once—The Roundabout Papers were, as you say, written at the club or in his own study or wherever he happened to be; and though he made various changes, as you notice, I think that on the whole they must also have been substantially written off-hand. He made, that is, no second copy, though probably the papers were simmering in his mind for some time.[22]

III

My subject, then, is Thackeray at work. It is an elusive activity which must often be reconstructed from glimpses, hunches, the circumstantial evidence of letters and unpublished manuscript materials. In this respect the authors of *Dickens at Work* had an inestimable advantage in Forster and the comprehensive Forster collection in the Victoria and Albert Museum. Thackeray had no confidential biographer, his working materials are many of them lost and all of them that survive, widely dispersed and there is, as yet, no complete edition of the letters. Evidence has to be taken where it can be found and this partly explains the method of the following chapters. There is no attempt to give an overall, substantial account of the composition of each of the major novels. Instead there are

9

offered a number of partial analyses illustrative of Thackeray's general manner of going about his work. The theme running throughout is that our author is a novelist of genius, but one whose genius is of a peculiarly spontaneous and easy-going nature.

I

VANITY FAIR
The Art of Improvisation

(1) THE IPHIGENIA SCENE

Unlike his other major works the composition of *Vanity Fair* has attracted a good deal of critical attention.[1] Rather than attempt a general picture, what is offered here are four snapshots of Thackeray at work on the novel. In them four units of structure are considered: the scene, the monthly number, the first three numbers and the whole novel. At each of these ascending levels we discover the same qualities of spontaneous invention and adaptation. This is not to say that Thackeray was an improviser and nothing else; as will appear he usually had a firm sense of the general direction his novel was taking. But below the level of what we may call the master-plan, Thackeray relied heavily on his powers of immediate invention and the characteristic 'touches of genius' were things of instantaneous creation.

We start with the closest snapshot of the four—the emergence on the manuscript sheet of a short but brilliant scene in Vanity Fair. Using the original draft we can see how when he is writing at his best Thackeray's narrative fizzes on the page as he enlarges, refines or complicates what he was about to say, often without so much as pausing in his rapid forward movement. The manuscript version of the scene is reproduced here (pl. 2)[2] together with Thackeray's own illustration for it (pl. 1). His handwriting may not be easily legible but I would ask the reader to look carefully at the autograph revisions. There follows the printed version of the scene:

. . . the utter silence in his genteel, well-furnished drawingroom, was only interrupted by the alarmed ticking of the great French clock.

When that chronometer, which was surmounted by a cheerful brass group of the sacrifice of Iphigenia, tolled five in a heavy cathedral tone, Mr. Osborne pulled the bell at his right hand violently, and the butler rushed up.

'Dinner!' roared Mr. Osborne.

'Mr. George isn't come in, sir,' interposed the man.

'Damn Mr. George, sir. Am I master of the house? DINNER!' Mr. Osborne scowled. Amelia trembled. A telegraphic communication of eyes passed between the other three ladies. The obedient bell in the lower regions began ringing the announcement of the meal. The tolling over, the head of the family thrust his hands into the great tail-pockets of his great blue coat and brass buttons, and without waiting for a further announcement, strode downstairs alone, scowling over his shoulder at the four females.

'What's the matter now, my dear?' asked one of the other, as they rose and tripped gingerly behind the sire.

'I suppose the funds are falling,' whispered Miss Wirt; and so, trembling and in silence, this hushed female company followed their dark leader. They took their places in silence. He growled out a blessing, which sounded as gruffly as a curse. The great silver dish-covers were removed. Amelia trembled in her place, for she was next to the awful Osborne, and alone on her side of the table—the gap being occasioned by the absence of George.

'Soup?' says Mr. Osborne, clutching the ladle, fixing his eyes on her, in sepulchral tone; and having helped her and the rest, did not speak for a while.

'Take Miss Sedley's plate away,' at last he said. 'She can't eat the soup—no more can I. It's beastly. Take away the soup, Hicks, and to-morrow turn the cook out of the house, Jane.'

Having concluded his observations upon the soup, Mr. Osborne made a few curt remarks respecting the fish, also of a savage and satirical tendency, and cursed Billingsgate with an emphasis quite worthy of the place. Then he lapsed into silence, and swallowed sundry glasses of wine, looking more and more terrible, till a brisk knock at the door told of George's arrival, when everybody began to rally.

'He could not come before. General Daguilet had kept him waiting at the Horse Guards. Never mind soup or fish. Give him anything —he didn't care what. Capital mutton—capital everything.' His good-humour contrasted with his father's severity; and he rattled on unceasingly during dinner, to the delight of all—of one especially, who need not be mentioned.

The reader will recognise the passage as one of the more famous moments in *Vanity Fair*, the first appearance of the Iphigenia clock. This ominous timepiece is introduced during an unlucky visit by Amelia Sedley to her *fiancé*'s house. Mr Sedley's business misfortunes have caused old Osborne to look askance on the girl he had arranged for his son George to marry and he makes no attempt to hide his disfavour from its terrified victim. Sacrifice is predicted by the very furniture around Amelia as the family, less George, prepare to take a wretched dinner.

The Iphigenia allusion is, one need hardly emphasise, felicitous. Figuratively it aptly foreshadows Amelia's fate while at the same time it triggers off a suggestive opposition between her as the passive Iphigenia victim and Becky as the active Clytemnestra: an opposition which is sustained until the murderous last chapter and 'Becky's second appearance in the character of Clytemnestra'. And this figurative richness is achieved without ever violating the literal likelihood of such an exotic ornament in Osborne's vulgarly 'well-furnished' drawing room.

The manuscript shows the emergence of this resonant detail

13

and the powerful scene around it as a series of elaborations vaulting rapidly one over another (all the corrections, incidentally, are in the same ink as the original). The kernel sentence seems to have been: 'When that chronometer tolled five in a heavy cathedral tone Mr. Osborne pulled the bell at his right hand violently, and the butler rushed up.' This, though neutral, was quite adequate and Thackeray could well have left it. But 'heavy cathedral tone' and 'tolled' with their suggestion of religious ritual seem to have inspired the ironic afterthought about 'the cheerful brass group of Jepththah sacrificing his daughter'. The parenthetic embellishment added to the effect but the overtone of biblical severity was not entirely appropriate to the old pagan Osborne, and the decoration was eccentric and extremely unlikely (it is also possible that Thackeray initially crossed out the line because he had misspelled 'Jephthah' as 'Jepththah'). Jephthah the Gileadite, the unlucky father forced to make a burnt offering of his only child because of a rash vow to God does not fit comfortably here. Nor was the syntax easy:

When that chronometer tolled five in a heavy cathedral tone, it had a cheerful brass group of Jephthah sacrificing his daughter, Mr. Osborne pulled the bell at his right hand violently, and the butler rushed up.

The problems were ironed out in the third stage of revision where Jephthah's daughter became Iphigenia sacrificed at Aulis. This made a number of happy concords. Stylistically it supports the Graecism 'chronometer' and in the matter of interior furnishing the 'great French clock' with its scene from *Iphigénie* is much more probable. The classical allusion also serves to alienate the cultivated narrator (and reader) from the vulgar Osborne who might well know his Old Testament but would certainly be ignorant of the Racine on his own mantelpiece.

Thackeray had at the same time contrived to unclutter the sentence order:

When that chronometer, which was surmounted by a cheerful brass group of the sacrifice of Iphigenia, tolled five in a heavy cathedral tone, Mr. Osborne pulled the bell at his right hand violently, and the butler rushed up.

One gets from the manuscript workings of this sentence a lively impression of rapid discovery, adaptation and improvement on discovery. Impressive too is Thackeray's restraint. In spite of its exciting possibilities he does not allow the Iphigenia allusion to become anything more than a grace-note. The point may be better appreciated if we compare it with the image-flogging in Trollope's chapter 11 of *The Warden*, 'Iphigenia', which is frankly derivative. Not that Thackeray neglected what had been so happily come upon. He took care to introduce Agamemnon into the left hand corner of his illustration and used the clock again as a grim commentary on the action in chapters 23 and 42.

II

The minor improvements in the scene—the mock-heroic 'lower regions' for 'down stairs', the addition of the 'blessing which sounded as gruffly as a curse' and the afterthought which placed Amelia 'next to the awful Osborne'—are self evident. The other major alteration is that which puts off George's arrival, thus prolonging the elder Osborne's loutish bullying of the harmless girl and his own less fragile womenfolk. On a dramatic level this corresponds with what the Iphigenia clock performs figuratively, that is to say it stresses the victimisation of Amelia by a cruel father figure. Again we can follow it as a flickering series of revisions which culminate in a brilliantly corrected passage. In the seventh paragraph it was first Thackeray's intention to fade the scene out with:

'Soup?' says Mr. Osborne fixing his eyes on her, in a sepulcral tone—but whether she took any or not does not matter for the purpose of this history.

But soup, he decided, did matter after all. The sentence was rewritten:

'Soup?' says Mr. Osborne fixing his eyes on her, in a sepulcral tone—and having helped her and the rest did not speak for a | LONG TIME | ⟨while⟩.

To this was added above as an afterthought the phrase 'clutching the ladle', a sinister description suggestive of the man's meanness: he is, in fact, intending just the opposite of hospitality as his hand grasps his dining-room silver. At this stage Thackeray again thought to end everyone's misery with the soup-course:

'Take away the soup Hicks' roared the master. At this moment came a brisk knock at the door. Succour had arrived and everybody began to rally.

But on second thoughts this was crossed out and relief postponed until the fish was come, cursed and gone; 'the master' being allowed to terrorise the company until the meal was half over. What he is thinking over his '| MANY | ⟨sundry⟩ glasses of wine' is made clear by the inserted 'tomorrow turn the cook out of the House Maria.'

The effect of twice delaying George's arrival is calculated, as is the exaggeration of Osborne's violence. Although this is the thirteenth chapter it is the merchant's first real appearance in the novel and Thackeray puts him before the reader in his full vulgarity and boorishness. And Osborne's brutality is not only seen, it is felt through the reader's sympathy with Amelia's misery. In this scene Thackeray manages wonderfully to communicate the silent throb of his heroine's passive suffering. The satire against the snobbish bully cross-cut with compassion for his victim demands a complex response from the reader, more complex, probably, than any demanded hitherto in the narrative.

Had Thackeray kept the original form of this scene with the unadorned French clock and George entering promptly with the soup there would have been no complaints. But the almost instantaneous flow of amendments creates a couple of those 'touches of genius' which seem sometimes to have surprised the novelist himself. The Iphigenia clock by a discreet and witty symbolism prophesies paternal tyranny: George's protracted absence allows full play for actual paternal tyranny at the dinner table. What began as a featureless stretch of connecting narrative has been transformed by deft retouching into a rich and compact scene.

(2) THE WATERLOO NUMBER

Most commentators would agree that Thackeray relied heavily on his powers of instant improvisation for the creation of scenes like that of the Iphigenia clock. But with regard to larger units—the number or the whole novel—there is disagreement about whether Thackeray planned or did not plan, or about how much of Trollope's 'elbow grease of the mind' (123) we may look for. The disagreement is neatly illustrated in the two major editions of *Vanity Fair* which have appeared in the last decade: Geoffrey and Kathleen Tillotson's (1963) and J. I. M. Stewart's (1968).[3] These editions, both admirable in their scholarship, put forward quite contrary views on Thackeray's craft. The Tillotsons argue for a conscientious novelist, one who protects his novel against the disintegrating pressures of serialisation by forethought: 'only the careful laying of ground in the early chapters,' they tell us, 'implying much premeditation of the subsequent course of the novel, could make possible such effective writing under such conditions' (xxi–xxiii). Stewart's Thackeray is quite other: 'those critics of the book who would vindicate *Vanity Fair* as a carefully pre-structured whole are really working against the grain of Thackeray's genius . . . the predominant feel of the book is one of brilliantly resourceful improvisation' (8).

The controversy here centres on the terms 'premeditation' and 'improvisation'. Is Thackeray's 'Novel without a Hero' what it is sometimes called a 'Novel without a Plan'? Those who set themselves to answer the question are handicapped by the lack of Thackeray's working materials for *Vanity Fair*. Apart from more or less casual remarks in letters (usually complaints about the pressure of deadlines) we know virtually nothing about the month-to-month writing of the novel. Hence on the purely subjective evidence of the work's 'feel' drastically opposite assessments are put forward. It is an unsatisfactory situation and one in which welcome light is thrown by a unique set of manuscript fragments and sketches in the Taylor collection at Princeton.[4] First look at the two pages of pencil drawings reproduced here (pls. 3–4). Next consider the following notes. They are all on separate pieces of what was obviously scrap paper, though the first two items probably were cut from the same page:

The bugles sounded the turnout, and you heard the assembly beating in various quarters of the town. The Major lost no time [In pencil on a small cut-out piece of paper, marbled on the reverse side indicating that it was, presumably, the inside leaf of a pocket book] in repairing to the alarm ground where he found men and officers hurrying from their billets [in pencil, on another small piece of paper apparently cut from the same sheet as the above].[5]

6   6

Jos with his servant
The state of the town 2½

Rebecca sells him the horses, etc. 3½   makes love to Jos

His flight Mrs. O'D's courage 2½

Dobbs return 1½   who will take care of him?
                                           I said Amelia

Quatre Bras 2½

These bits and pieces give us a brief but unique insight into Thackeray's working methods. They refer, of course, to Number 9 of *Vanity Fair*, the highly complicated and justly famous Waterloo chapters. The first two written items belong to the beginnings of chapter 30 and the serio-comic description of Major and Mrs O'Dowd's preparations for the impending battle. This is how the scene forecast in the jottings inside the cover of the unknown pocket book finally reached print:

. . . Mrs. O'Dowd woke up her Major, and had as comfortable a cup of coffee prepared for him as any made that morning in Brussels. And who is there will deny that this worthy lady's preparations betokened affection as much as the fits of tears and hysterics by which more sensitive females exhibited their love, and that their partaking of this coffee, which they drank together while *the bugles were sounding the turn-out and the drums beating in the various quarters of the town*, was not more useful and to the purpose than the outpouring of any mere sentiment could be? The consequence was, that *the Major appeared on parade* quite trim, fresh, and alert, his well-shaved rosy countenance, as he sate on horseback, giving cheerfulness and confidence to the whole corps. (283–4, my italics)

The third of these fragments shows Thackeray measuring out the proportions of an as yet unwritten part of his novel. Such calculations are to be found elsewhere in his manuscript notes and were particularly important for the serialist filling a prescribed number of pages each month. Though neither his handwriting nor his writing paper were, until late in life, metrically consistent, Thackeray obviously kept a running account of his novel's quantities as he went along. Hence such computation as this in the *Duval* notebook:[6]

> my page holds 24 lines.
> 4 Ms lines = 5 of print.
> 24 lines = 30 of print.
> 30 Ms pages = 24 of print.
> 5 Ms pages = 4 print.
> $1\frac{1}{2}$ pages = 1p of print.

But we may make other than simply quantitative deductions from the *Vanity Fair* schedule. What we have there are the propositions for two chapters of about 6 double MS. pages each. These finally appeared as chapters 31 and 32 but in their published form, although recognisable, they are significantly different. This can be best shown if we convert the finished chapters back to the kind of synopsis shorthand Thackeray originally used:

Chapter 31	Chapter 32
Jos with his servant Isidor	Jos's terror: he shaves his whiskers
The state of the town	Rebecca snubs Lady Bareacres
Rebecca makes love to Jos	Rebecca sells Jos the horses
Rebecca visits Amelia	Stubble returns wounded: Mrs. O'D will take care of him
	Jos's flight. Mrs. O'D's anger
	Quatre Bras

A moment's comparison shows the discrepancies between

plan and execution. Jos's interview with Rebecca is broken into two, a split anticipated in Thackeray's apparently parenthetic 'makes love to Jos'. Lovemaking becomes the business of their first meeting, horsetrading of the second. The effect of the enlargement is to stress the comedy of Jos's military bravado and ultimate ignominious flight and to create an overarching episode which contains the rest. Towards the same end the delightfully funny 'Coupez-moi' scene was introduced.

Surprisingly we see that at first Thackeray intended to make much more of the 'great battle' by giving a climactic two and a half pages (almost half a chapter) to Quatre Bras. In the event he declined to play the 'military novelist' and offered only half a page of muted and general comment, concentrating instead on its domestic repercussions. The understatement was, it is generally acknowledged, a master-stroke.[7]

Other rebalancings followed the novelist's non-combatant role. Becky was promoted to having, with Jos, the lead part in this sequence. Thackeray added the hypocritical sisterly visit to Amelia and the lighter business of her mischievously tantalising the horseless, but relentlessly snobbish, Bareacres. These additions to the original scheme, and others, are reflected in the two sheets of pencil sketches. There we can detect the packed rucksack denoting the departed soldiers, Becky's pretty head in untroubled slumber as her husband marches off to possible death (this was actually worked up to illustrate chapter 30), the ill-fated whiskers (not on Jos but Isidor who daydreams about himself in his master's finery) and the unharnessed Bareacres coach with its prominent aristocratic lozenge. It is probable, though not provable, that Thackeray created this little montage of afterthought material before or while he was writing the chapters: that what we have here is Thackeray playing with ideas for his evolving novel.

We are on less speculative ground with the last and most

intriguing of the deviations from the little plan—that concerning 'Dobbs return' and 'who will take care of him—I said Amelia'. In accordance with the decision to enclose the chapters in Jos's rise and fall as a military man this scene (in altered form) was advanced to before the fat hero's flight. It was also played down. No such heroic self-sacrifice as that implied in 'I said Amelia' is in fact portrayed. Indeed the juvenile Ensign Stubble is looked after by the more motherly Mrs O'Dowd:

'And—and you won't leave me, will you, Mrs. O'Dowd?'
'No, my dear fellow,' said she, going up and kissing the boy. 'No harm shall come to you while *I* stand by' (313).

We note, however, that originally Thackeray did not intend the wounded man to be the boyish Ensign Stubble but 'Dobb'. 'Dobb' or 'Dob' is, of course, Dobbin's nickname.[8] It seems that a wounded Dobbin (deliriously raving his love?) was to have been nursed by a heroic Amelia who had given up her chance of safe passage with Jos to do so. Meanwhile George was to fall at Quatre Bras.

It would be pointless to ask whether the events Thackeray eventually decided on for his novel are an improvement or not. The original shape of things would have injected more life into the subsequent *longueurs* of the Amelia–Dobbin relationship if, albeit unconsciously, he had declared his criminal affection for Mrs Osborne while George was still alive; and it would have given more point to the years-long exile in India. But, demonstrably, Thackeray had decided to cool down his account of the Waterloo crisis and as part of this process Amelia and Dobbin were to be allowed no contact.

II

This set of thumbnail and probably incomplete notes for *Vanity Fair* is uniquely informative about Thackeray's methods. The uniqueness lies in the fact that they concern the central narrative line of the novel and that they show Thackeray inventing, outlining, measuring, altering, experimenting—going through all the functions we associate with planning. Admittedly the planning is of an extremely flexible and provisional kind, but one senses that it was a habitual exercise. Thackeray was lamentably indifferent about his manuscript materials and so were his family executors. When most of the *Vanity Fair* manuscript is lost one appreciates that only a lucky freak preserved the foregoing set of notes. Bearing this in mind it is not unjustifiable to assume the kind of preparatory work which goes into the Waterloo chapters elsewhere in the novel, and in Thackeray's fiction generally.

(3) THE 'VANITY FAIR' INTERPOLATIONS

The surviving manuscript of *Vanity Fair* is much revised, and the nature of the revisions is complex and controversial. There is general agreement, however, that up to the twelfth chapter there are two and possibly three layers of work—that *Vanity Fair*, in other words, rests on the shaky foundation of an unwritten other novel. These layers correspond to three distinct periods of composition which may be given probable, but no more than probable, dates. The earliest is spring 1845 when the group of chapters 1–4, 6A and a continuation, parts of which finally found their way into the printed chapters 8 and 9, were written.[9] Next we have the layer apparently dating from summer 1846 when chapter 5 and the second version of 6 were added, thus introducing Dobbin and altering the character of Osborne. The third discernible layer (and of course there is much in these early chapters which is not easily placed) belongs to autumn 1846 when Thackeray seems to have inserted a number of sententious apostrophes to 'Vanity Fair' into his already written narrative. The date of this third layer is, in fact, more definite than those of the other two since it is recorded that Thackeray hit on the novel's Bunyanesque title late in 1846[10] (it will be noted that he did not work the 'Vanity Fair' theme properly into the novel until after the first hundred pages were past).

Gordon Ray was the first to draw attention to these after-thought passages of moral commentary and the way in which they transform the novel. Without them we would have, he asserts, 'a detached noncommittal narrative in which the reader is told what happened, but rarely what to think about it'.[11] The 'Vanity Fair' interpolations are cited by Ray, together with massive biographical evidence, to show that the novelist underwent a revolutionary 'change of heart' in 1846.[12] He settled with his family, moderated his formerly nihilistic and savage misanthropy into more reasonable attitudes and began to practise his profession in a spirit as 'serious as the parson's own'.[13] The earlier layers of *Vanity Fair* were, then, refurbished by a changed man and, Ray believes, a greater novelist for the change. The refurbishing takes the form not of re-writing but of enveloping the opening chapters in the moral outlook he conceived later and this is achieved by the simple expedient of three crucially inserted 'sermonings' on 'Vanity Fair' around the chapter 8–9 area.[14]

Ray's theory of the split composition of *Vanity Fair* is brilliant and clear cut, but in some ways it may be found too clear cut. The Tillotsons, for example, modify the point about the original narrative spareness of the 1–4, 6A chapters, pointing out several passages where the 'reader is told what to think'. Another, rather humdrum, modification may be added; namely the possibility that Thackeray, used to the clipped dimensions of the magazine serial (and perhaps thinking of this outlet for his present story) found that he was burning up material too fast and added the apostrophes to plump out his narrative. The convenient ease with which he could, on such occasions, 'sermonise' is notorious. Examining *Vanity Fair* with this in mind one notes that the chapters are, on average, ten pages long. Chapters 8 and 9, where the insertions occur, have only fourteen pages between them—twelve without the additional material. In their original form they are, then, slightly too long for a single chapter and too short for two chapters. It is at least possible that the apostrophes are less a *cri de coeur* than the early exercises in a narrative upholstery which was to become Thackeray's stock in trade. They may be there less to 'tell the reader what to think' than to furnish some needed bulk.

Some support for this view may be found in chapter 7. This chapter does not exist in manuscript and was almost certainly written later than the layers we are talking about, perhaps even after the first number had gone to the printer. Chapter 7 recounts at amusing length Becky's journey to Gaunt Square, the rudeness of John the footman, the surprising apparition of the baronet as a grubby boor, Becky's having to sleep with the housekeeper and to ride outside the carriage on the journey to Hampshire—discomfort made easier by the young man from Cambridge. Now all this information which is spun out in chapter 7 is contained in the first four paragraphs of Becky's letter which opens the third number (Chapter 8). What Thackeray seems to have done in chapter 7 is to inflate a portion of Becky's narrative (repeating himself while so doing) so as to avoid pushing his story on too fast.

II

It will be objected that this does not answer for the key issue which is one of tone and commitment. Do the 'Vanity Fair' insertions really show a revised version of the 'novelist's responsibility'? Here again Ray's clear argument is more doubtful on close investigation. Take the longest and most complex of the apostrophes in its full form and context. It is attached to the end of chapter 8 after Becky's spiteful letter about her employers at Queen's Crawley. These then with the important crossings-out and breaks are what, according to Ray, should be taken as 'six concluding paragraphs which sum up the serious and responsible view that [Thackeray] had come to take of novel-writing':[15]

Everything considered, I think it is quite as well for our dear Amelia Sedley in Russell Square, that Miss Sharp and she are parted. Rebecca is a droll funny creature to be sure; and those descriptions of the poor lady weeping for the loss of her beauty, and the gentleman 'with hay-coloured whiskers and straw-coloured hair' are very smart doubtless and show a great deal of knowledge of the world. That she might when on her knees have been thinking of something better than Miss Horrocks's ribbons has possibly struck both of us. But my kind reader will please to remember, that these histories in their gaudy yellow covers, have 'Vanity Fair' for a title and that Vanity Fair is a very vain wicked foolish place, full of all sorts of humbugs and falsenesses and pretensions. | YOU SEE TOO BY THE PICTURE OUTSIDE THAT THE MORALIST WHO IS HOLDING FORTH ON THE COVER IS DRESSED IN THE VERY SAME LONG-EARED LIVERY WHICH HIS AUDIENCE SPORTS AND PROFESSES TO BE NO BETTER THAN THEY ὄιη περ φυλλῶν γένεα τοιαδε καὶ ἀνδρῶν. |[16] [The Greek quotation is deleted in the MS.] And while the moralist who is holding forth on the cover (an accurate portrait of your humble servant) professes to wear neither gown nor bands, but only the very same long-eared livery in which his congregation is arrayed; yet, look you, one is bound to speak the truth as far as one knows it, whether one mounts a cap and bells or a shovel-hat, and a deal of disagreeable matter must come out in the course of such an undertaking. | WHEN CAPTAIN BEAUFORT AND CAPTAIN BECHER MAKE CHARTS AT THE

ADMIRALTY, THEY SET DOWN THE ROCKS CREEKS BAYS QUICKSANDS IN THEIR PROPER PLACES OR THE DEUCE WOULD BE IN IT AND THE UNWARY MARINER WOULD FIND HIMSELF STRIKING ON A BAR OR FLOUNDERING ON A QUICKSAND WHERE HE HAD BEEN LED TO EXPECT A CLEAR CHANNEL AND DEEP WATER SO IN OUR | [The sentence breaks off and there is a break of a third of a page.]

I have heard a brother of the story-telling trade at Naples, preaching to a pack of good for nothing honest lazy fellows by the sea-shore, work himself up into such a rage and passion with some of the villains whose wicked deeds he was describing and inventing, that the audience could not resist it, and they and the poet together would burst out into a roar of oaths and execrations against the fictitious monster of the tale, so that the hat went round and the bajocchi tumbled into it in the midst of a perfect storm of sympathy.

At the little Paris theatres on the other hand you will not only hear the people yelling out Ah gredin Ah monstre! and cursing the tyrant of the play from the boxes; but the actors themselves positively refuse to play the wicked parts, such as those of *infâmes Anglais* brutal Cossacks and what not, and prefer to appear at a smaller salary in their real characters as loyal Frenchmen. I set the two stories one against the other, so that you may see that it is not from mere mercenary motives that the present performer is desirous to show up and trounce his villains, but because he has a sincere hatred of them which he cannot keep down, and which must find a vent in suitable abuse and bad language.

I warn 'my kyind friends' then, that I am going to tell a story of harrowing villainy and complicated but as I trust intensely interesting crime. My rascals are no milk and water rascals I promise you. When we come to the proper places we wont spare fine language no no—as when we are going over the quiet country we must perforce be calm. A tornado in a slop basin is absurd. We will reserve that sort of thing for the mighty ocean and the lonely midnight. The present Number will be very mild. Others—But we will not anticipate *those*.

And as we bring our characters forward, I will ask leave as a man and a brother, not only to introduce them, but occasionally to step down from the | STAGE | ⟨platform⟩ and talk about them. If they are good and kindly, to love them and shake them by the hand; if they are silly to laugh at them confidentially in the reader's sleeve: if they are wicked and heartless to abuse them in the strongest terms which politeness admits of.

Otherwise you might fancy it was I who was sneering at the practice of devotion, which Miss Sharp finds so ridiculous; that it was I who laughed good-humouredly at the reeling old Silenus of a baronet—whereas the laughter comes from one who has no reverence except for prosperity and no eye for anything beyond success. Such people there are living and flourishing in the world—Faithless Hopeless Charityless—let us have at them dear friends with might and main. Some there are, and very successful too, mere quacks and fools—it was to combat and expose such as those no doubt, that Laughter was made.

Superficially it seems like a confidence to the reader *in propria persona*, Harlequin without the paint, a glimpse of 'the sentimental gentleman ... under the mask satirical'.[17] Yet if one follows the tracery of allusion and self-mockery, one's response is much more vexed. In the first paragraph Thackeray originally intended to wind up with a piece of Homeric pessimism but he changed his mind and instead elaborated the headgear joke—'long-eared livery ... cap and bells ... shovel hat'. The allusion is to Carlyle's essay 'Biography' (*Fraser's Magazine*, 27 April 1832) and is tendentious. Carlyle's essay is largely an attack on fiction and its generic 'untruths'. Fifty years later this blast against the 'Novelwright' and his 'long-ear of a Fictitious Biography' was still felt by Trollope as a painful aspersion on the profession which needed to be put down.[18] Here Thackeray's main point 'one must speak the truth as far as one knows it'—that is, novelists must be reliable in their moral commentary—is clear enough and Carlylean enough.

But it is odd to utter it in the person of Carlyle's jester and by so doing apparently acquiesce (as Trollope refuses to do) in the derogatory image. The ass-eared fool is, *sui generis*, unreliable and the effect of the impersonation here is to undermine the credibility of the protestations about 'truth'.

The next explanatory image Thackeray broke off and crossed out leaving the rest of the page blank. The suppressed analogy, a neat one, refines the train of thought by suggesting the narrator should act as a moral cartographer, providing reliable bearings for the reader. Why, one wonders, did Thackeray break it off? The next paragraph beginning 'I have heard a brother of the story-telling trade at Naples . . .' starts a fresh manuscript page and seems to have been taken from a different draft. For the train of thought is suddenly turned about. Thackeray here and in the third paragraph satirises the absolute *unreliability* of the involved artist's commentary on his creation, whether for commercial or subjective emotional reasons. Trust the tale not the teller, ignore authorial maps he seems now to say. It is all very perplexing.

But the reader is not allowed to linger on any suspicion that Thackeray is paltering with him in double sense. One image flickers over another. The mercenary raconteur and his audience logically suggests another kind of Latin excitability, that of the Paris theatre where actors and audience whip each other into ludicrous partisanship. Again the analogy is hardly flattering to the narrator intending to 'show up and trounce his villains' or to 'tell his reader what to think.'

By another logical jump, bad French theatre suggests bad English. 'I warn "my kyind friends"' mimics the then manager of Drury Lane, Alfred Bunn. 'The poet Bunn', a favourite butt of Thackeray and his *Punch* associates in the 1840s, was notorious for his maudlin habit of coming down to the front of stage to address his 'kind friends', the audience, over the foots. It was a spectacle Thackeray and his satirical colleagues claimed to find nauseating.

The last two paragraphs follow the same kind of free-associative course. Thackeray, still vaguely in the character of Showman Bunn, introduces his troupe saying he will step down from the platform (originally 'stage') to confer with his reader about the onstage action giving him reliable pointers as to what to think. But the imposture, as did the long-eared livery, undermines what he is saying. One's suspicions as to the narrator's seriousness are also aroused by two loaded expressions: 'a man and a brother' and 'in the strongest terms which politeness admits of'. *Am I not a man and a brother?*—the abolitionist's slogan, was used so often by Thackeray that it can be considered a catchphrase and like other catchphrases it normally signals that Thackeray is not quite serious. Here it carries the mock-humble overtone that Thackeray is a slave of the pen and its flippant wittiness suggests that we should not hunt for any great moral significance. Likewise with the other phrase, 'in the strongest terms which politeness admits of'; this is merely riddling because in *Vanity Fair* politeness admits of no strong terms whatsoever. The point is made for us at the beginning of chapter 64: 'a polite public will no more bear to read an authentic description of vice than a truly-refined English or American female will permit the word breeches to be pronounced in her chaste hearing' (617). This entertaining, if bewildering sequence is finally cut off with a pious adaptation of the apostle's eulogy of charity.

The six paragraphs give us, for the first time, the intricately wrought frame of the novel—*Vanity Fair*, narrative harlequinade, the presiding showman pointing, nudging, laughing in our sleeve. These are all stored away to be worked into the magnificent preface cum *envoi* 'Before the Curtain'. But taken altogether here the passage is extraordinarily riddled with self-inflicted irony. It begins by the narrator invoking and voluntarily donning the fool's uniform Carlyle designed for the novelist and those who are taken in by his deceits. It then gives two telling examples of the fatuity of taking sides for or against fictional characters. Next, in the borrowed person of a dramatic impresario he despised, Thackeray nonetheless says not only that he *will* take sides but that he wants his *parti pris* to be unequivocal. Momentarily he blacks his face in mock-slavish humility and offers the paradoxical assurance that his criticism will be 'in the strongest terms politeness admits of' which in the mealy mouthed world of *Vanity Fair* means no terms at all. And the chapter ends with a repudiation of 'Miss Sharp'— the 'Becky' and 'our heroine' of earlier pages.

It is not, we may conclude, an easy passage. One applauds the agility but in some ways his moral purposes would have been better served had he simply kept the Fieldingesque sentence which originally followed Becky's letter in the manuscript and which was crossed out to give way to the subsequent tirade: 'Miss Sharp's opinions with regard to the two young ladies whom she was to instruct was made with her usual intelligence and fine feeling.' As it is rewritten one glides over six paragraphs with a vague sense that one is getting nearer to Thackeray and his intention but the final effect is mystification. The mystification is familiar enough to the seasoned reader: Thackeray loves to 'change a visor quicker than thought' revealing in the change not his face but another mask. But such virtuosity hardly makes for the simple communication of a 'serious and responsible view ... of novel writing'.

Gordon Ray is certainly right about the 'change of heart'. But far from enabling Thackeray with new confidence the change, I suspect, landed him in an artistic impasse which, as here, he could only blur with a distractingly virtuosic display. It is clear that a large part of the impasse concerned 'Miss Sharp' as she is now frigidly called. What does it mean he will 'have at her with might and main'? How do we square this with his proclaimed habit of letting characters lead him, not he them? How do we reconcile this proposed moral battery with such tributes as Professor Tillotson's that 'Becky swims free in the pure element of art'[19] or Thackeray's own comments in later life to J. E. Cooke?

I like Becky in that book. Sometimes I think I have myself some of her tastes. I like what are called Bohemians and fellows of that sort. I have seen all sorts of society—dukes, duchesses, lords and ladies, authors and actors and painters—and taken altogether I think I like painters the best, and Bohemians generally.[20]

As regards the 'Vanity Fair' apostrophes and particularly the major one at the end of chapter 8 it seems reasonable to suggest that before being read as credos about fiction and life they should be considered as running repair work to a novel which was rapidly outgrowing its original frame and moving its moral standpoint. This activity is physically apparent from a great deal of scissors and paste work around the manuscript chapters 6 to 10, and as we have seen Thackeray may have been concerned at the same time to decelerate his narrative generally. But more important than any quantitative considerations are the realignments between narrator and dramatis personae which we see taking place and which are closely tied in with the mode of narration. Apart from its last six paragraphs chapter 8 is epistolary, recounted by a savage and vivacious Becky. Many readers must have wondered why, in fact, Thackeray flirts with the epistolary form in this section and then drops it for good. The reason seems to have been an original intention to make extensive use of the witty heroine's correspondence. But Thackeray later came to feel that he had to divorce his narration from Becky's, indeed oust her altogether as a narrator (though typically he was too thrifty with his effort to throw away all of what he had written through her). This severance was made absolute by the authorial afterword to chapter 8 in which a key sentence is, surely: 'otherwise you might fancy it was I who was sneering at the practice of devotion, which Miss Sharp finds so ridiculous' (81).

A lesser novelist might have gone on to 'trounce' Becky as threatened. What such action would have meant for the novel in general is evident from a couple of small examples where Thackeray can be seen momentarily yielding to the impulse. The first is taken, again, from the manuscript of chapter 8 and Becky's coach ride to Queen's Crawley:

. . . the young gentleman made me remark that we drove very slow for the last two stages on the road, because Sir Pitt was on the box, and because he is proprietor of the horses for this part of the journey. 'But wont I flog 'em on to Squashmore when I take the ribbons' said the young *Cantab*. 'And sarve 'em right, Master Jack' said the guard. When I comprehended the meaning of this phrase, and that Master Jack intended to drive the rest of the way, of course I interceded for the poor animals.

The last part of this Thackeray altered to:

When I comprehended the meaning of this phrase, and that Master Jack intended to drive the rest of the way, and revenge himself on Sir Pitt's horses, of course I laughed too. (75)

The alteration is crude and improbable. In writing to Amelia Becky would quite likely affect hypocritical compassion for flogged horses; she would never be fool enough, nor brute enough one suspects, to display a relish for animal suffering to a correspondent who 'would cry over a dead canary bird' (15). What Thackeray does here is to distort Becky so as to alienate

33

the reader and render him more disposed and her more accessible to 'trouncing'.

The other example is famous—Becky's slapping her young son's face for stealing down to hear her sing. Lord David Cecil comments: 'Now people of her temperament neglect their children, but their very selfishness makes them good-natured to them. And Becky in particular was so avid of admiration that she would have been pleased that anyone should enjoy her singing.'[21] Cecil's explanation of this and similar lapses is, I think, correct:

These inconsistencies in character are Thackeray's most serious fault. But one can understand why he committed them. They are due to the influence of the age in which he lived. The militant moral views that ruled every aspect of Victorian life with so tyrannical a sway, were not ultimately consistent with that moral order whose creation is the centre of Thackeray's artistic achievement.[22]

In other words Thackeray the public moralist and Thackeray the artist could not always keep time. But lapses like this are rare and Gordon Ray is surely correct, in his turn, when he claims that Thackeray developed a practice of socially responsible artistry to harmonise these elements in his mature fiction and that, like so much else, this practice is perfected in the first hundred-or-so pages of *Vanity Fair*. But where Ray's argument seems questionable is in its insistence that the apostrophes in themselves *represent* this new responsibility. It is less a matter of being than doing: and it seems to me that what the three passages do, and especially the crucial one we have looked at, is to roughly elbow out space by distancing the narrator from the action and, more particularly, from Becky. By so doing they help accommodate a fuller and subtler interplay between the action and the observing moral consciousness, the 'Fair' and the 'man with a reflective turn of mind' (5).

34

(4) TIME AND THE NOVEL

In this fourth section we consider the function of improvisation in a still larger context—the handling of time in the novel as a whole. Chronology posed serious problems for Thackeray who had never before tackled a work on the scale of *Vanity Fair*. Successful adaptation came late and only after some narrative discomfort. In the course of the novel we can detect a process of trial and error and in the early sections particularly, more error than Thackeray can have been happy with. Yet the problem was eventually solved, and solved by a characteristic reliance on quick narrative reflexes.

The first thing one notices in considering the time-scheme of *Vanity Fair* is how disproportionate the overall arrangement is. Of its six-hundred-odd pages three hundred are given to the two years before Waterloo, the other three hundred to the twenty-five years after it: the first half of the novel is compact, the second sprawling. For convenience the pre-Waterloo half can be sub-divided into two further segments, those of the unmarried and the honeymoon careers of the heroines or in terms of dates: summer 1813 to winter 1814, spring 1815 to summer 1815. In the first of these Thackeray's identification of events against calendar time is meticulous and exact. In the second it is still close but such punctiliousness is clearly beginning to embarrass him. In the third of the novel's eras, Waterloo onwards, there emerges a studied vagueness about dating which suggests that the novelist has gauged his readership's indifference to chronological precision and is taking full artistic advantage of it.

The novel begins with promising exactitude: 'While the present century was in its teens, and on one sunshiny morning in June . . .' (11). In the following hundred pages we learn that

35

Rebecca is to stay ten days with the Sedleys, that she is nineteen years old and Amelia seventeen, that Jos is twelve years older than his sister, that George is twenty-three and Dobbin five years his senior, that the year coyly given as the 'teens' of the century must be 1813 and that the 'sunshiny morning in June' is the 15th. Thackeray's chronometer is heard clearly in these early well-planned pages.

There are, however, significant gaps after Becky goes to take up her new position as governess at Queen's Crawley in July 1813. We learn that she soon ingratiates herself with the boorish baronet and his household. She herself tells Amelia this in her second letter (her first is begun the day of her arrival) which opens: 'I have not written to my beloved Amelia for these many weeks [MS. |MONTHS|] past . . .' (98). This is undated but juxtaposed with a snooping letter from Mrs Bute Crawley dated 'December —'. The position and contents of these letters make it clear they belong to December 1813–January 1814 shortly after Becky has settled in. In this same letter Becky reports the annual visit of the 'great rich Miss Crawley' with whom, we gather, the new governess promptly becomes a favourite, as she does with the dandy Rawdon who follows everywhere in his aunt's entourage.

There follow two intervening chapters which cover, with great generality, 'fifteen or eighteen months' (113) during which Amelia languishes for a heartless George. Then we have chapter 14 which opens: 'About this time there drove up to an exceedingly snug and well-appointed house in Park Lane, a travelling chariot with a lozenge on the panels' (127). The carriage contains Becky and a sick Miss Crawley 'returning from Hants'. Arrived in London Becky immediately ousts Miss Briggs as companion while that less designing spinster is enjoying her 'Christmas revels in the elegant home of my firm friends, the Reverend Lionel Delamere and his amiable

lady' (129). This action is obviously intended to be consecutive
with the December 1813 visit which Becky described in her
letter. But, in a sense, it cannot be. For hard on Miss Crawley's
cure a few weeks after, Becky secretly marries and elopes with
Rawdon ('six weeks . . . had victimised him completely' [132])
and this is demonstrably sometime around February 1815. What
Thackeray has done is coolly to remove a year out of Becky's
life: for her as for the whole 'Arcadian' set 1814 simply does not
happen—they go direct to 1815. So Becky is reunited in London
with her friend of 'last year' (138), Amelia, having won over
Rawdon and Miss Crawley on the first, not second, encounter.

The reasons for the time jump are fairly clear: the passive
Amelia may mark time for a year and a half doing nothing but
pine for the man of her dreams, active Becky may not. It
touches on a problem which Thackeray faces throughout
Vanity Fair, namely that Becky does so much more with her
time than Amelia that in any truly parallel treatment she would
monopolise the narrative. The solution, as here, is to black
out by one means or another sections of the adventuress-
heroine's life so that her sprints only serve to keep her abreast
of Amelia's 'insufferably tedious' (553) marathon.[23] There is
also, as we know, another reason for the missing year out of
Becky's life. Thackeray originally intended to give us a much
fuller account of Becky's intrigues at Queen's Crawley. He also
intended a more complex social arrangement during Miss
Crawley's visits. The end of the MS. chapter 9 has this deleted
tailpiece:

Twice a year a big carriage drawn by fat horses driven by a fat
coachman (the establishment of maiden ladies is always fat) used to
drive up the avenue to Queen's Crawley and turn into the abode of ▪
the worthy rector of that parish.[24]

In the final abbreviated version Miss Crawley visits the country

37

once a year, at Christmas, and stays with the senior branch of the family. The intricate rivalries and jockeying for preference which the deleted passage predicts were, with Becky's intrigues, simplified and shortened.

Such alterations were, we know, common enough in Thackeray's fiction. But what is uncommon in these early, well chronicled, pages of *Vanity Fair* is that by reference to his own chronological information we can catch Thackeray out in what seems like a clumsy piece of narrative syncopation. Becky's missing year snags one's pleasure irritatingly in the opening numbers—assuming, of course, that one notices it.

II

The section between the heroines' marriages and Waterloo, May to mid-June 1815, is the most complicated and tight-knit in the novel, chronologically speaking. So much happens in the way of making new marital relationships and breaking old family ones that Thackeray barely manages to get his characters to Brussels in time for the battle. And his habit of moving backwards and forwards rather than in a straight line of narrative produces something very like a tangle when the action must be synchronised with a close timetable. This is most easily shown by a summary of the events of May 1815.

We enter the month with this lead-in:

> Some ten days after the above ceremony, three young men of our acquaintance were enjoying that beautiful prospect of bow windows on the one side and blue sea on the other, which Brighton affords to the traveller. (208)

The three young men are Jos, George and Rawdon; the 'ceremony' is George's wedding which took place 'at the end of April' (205)—the 25th as we later learn.[25] This, then, gives us a date of about May 4 for the above scene. The young men walk along to meet the London coach which delivers Dobbin returning as an unsuccessful envoy to George's father. The narrative loops back for a chapter to follow this episode centring on Dobbin's announcement to old Osborne that George 'married Miss Sedley five days ago' (221) which, if we are pedantic enough to calculate, means that the interview occurs in the last days of April. The day after this Mr Osborne writes a dismissive letter to his son which is given to Dobbin to hand over. When this is opened we discover that it is dated 'May 7' (231), at least a week in the future.

Chapter 25 brings us up to Dobbin's arrival again, his gloomy tidings and the dinner that night at the Ship Inn. But in describing the woes of Amelia Thackeray takes us back once more to 'the night before Dobbin came' (234) when, we are told, 'scarce a week was past' since the wedding which, give or take a couple of days, is the most accurate time correlation we have from Thackeray in this section. The Osbornes leave Brighton for London the day after Dobbin's arrival and that same evening Amelia goes to visit her mother in Fulham, an occasion for nostalgic retrospection: 'There were but nine days past since Amelia had left that little cottage and home—and yet how far off the time seemed since she had bidden it farewell' (250). If we are to believe the 'ten days' (208) reference of a day earlier it should indeed seem far off.

The fact is that it irks Thackeray to work in such close confines and, worse than this, it makes him seem clumsy, careless and arrogant about details. Clearly he felt so himself for in chapter 25 he offers this apology:

Our history is destined in this chapter to go backwards and forwards in a very irresolute manner seemingly, and having conducted our story to to-morrow presently, we shall immediately again have occasion to step back to yesterday, so that the whole of the tale may get a hearing. (234)

It is not, in context, a suave aside but a self-conscious acknowledgement of the inartistic congestion which telling the story according to a close schedule has involved him in. Thackeray was bogged down in his narrative. His letters show that he aimed to get to Waterloo by the seventh number (in the event the battle had to wait until the end of the ninth.)[26] At the same time we feel Thackeray straining for effects which need years, not the months which his tight chronological scheme allows. The reader may appreciate these effects only by a kind of self-imposed myopia. Take, as a representative instance, this comment by Gordon Ray:

Thackeray's perspective makes him particularly expert in bringing out the design of individual lives and of human life generally. Consider, for example, the career of old Mr. Sedley. Early in the novel he emerges for a time from Thackeray's vast panorama. We see a hearty, coarse-grained, jovial man, sure of himself and flushed with success, ordering about his wife and daughter and making his son uncomfortable with his rough jokes. He disappears for a dozen chapters. When we encounter him again, years have passed, his business has failed, and he has become the broken-down frequenter of a third-rate City coffee-house,

> Familiar as an old mistake
> And futile as regret.[27]

Fifteen chapters have passed, *years* have not. Twenty-one months are all that has elapsed between the 'jovial' Sedley of chapter 4 and the coffee-house frequenter of chapter 20. But we feel Ray is right: Sedley *is* years older in the Tapioca Coffee-house. It is simply that by Thackeray's chronological account we cannot find the years which have transformed him.

It is at about this stage in the novel that the novelist seems to have realised that cramping narrative scale and scrupulous notation of time did not suit a story-teller of his expansive inclinations. For after Waterloo the narrative is relaxed and extended to the dimensions which we normally consider characteristic of Thackeray's mature fiction.

The tone and scope of the novel's new larger-scale organisation is given when after the victory we are told that the Crawleys stay 'some two or three years' at Paris, 'of which we can afford to give but a very brief history' (351). Two years has been the sum of the whole history up to this point. As striking as the larger perspective, however, is the vagueness of 'some two or three years'. Thackeray ceases to be the exact chronicler and becomes the great novelist. The importance of what happens at this middle stage is not always appreciated. Praise like the following is, strictly speaking, appropriate only to the second half of the novel or, to put it another way, the novel as it is enlarged by its second half:

Vanity Fair is his first novel on a big scale, and it is a great novel because its big space is scrupulously occupied. For all its immensity, it works under a statute of limitation. There is no fat on its mammoth frame. (v)

Had Thackeray died half way through *Vanity Fair* as he did half way through *Denis Duval* few would have foreseen a novel deserving the Tillotsons' description. Lengthy perhaps, but not big.

The epic size and magnificent ease of the novel as it continues seem intimately connected with a disdain for chronological precision. From Waterloo to the end of the work only a few firm dates are given: little Rawdon's birth on 26 March 1816, old Sir Pitt's death on 14 September 1822, Dobbin's return to England in spring 1827, the summer holiday at Pumpernickel in 1830. These are the few reference points which we have in trying to draw up a calendar for the post-1815 action. Consequently it is, for example, impossible to put dates to the crop of deaths which occur as the years go by and most of the important scenes can be fixed only approximately. But there are practical advantages for Thackeray. Imprecision and the need for much larger tracts of time to be covered mean that he does not have to calculate which day, month or even year it is as he goes 'backwards and forwards' in his story— hence there is no more of that clumsiness which mars the seventh number. The larger scale and vaguer time reference also mean that Thackeray can perpetrate anachronisms without disconcerting the reader or embarrassing himself and this is useful in achieving the effects he desires.

In order to show this it is again necessary to follow a maze of contradictory dates, but ones which do not stand out so indiscreetly. For example we can only deduce as a probability that Becky and Rawdon return to England in late 1817. When Rawdon breaks open his wife's escritoire the night he surprises her alone with Steyne he finds that 'she has kep[t] money concealed from me these ten years' (537), which confirms the impression that Becky's years of triumph in society are 1825–1827. But if this is the case how does one explain landlord Raggles' woeful complaints after the crash?

'Har you a goin' to pay me? You've lived in this 'ouse four year. You've 'ad my substance: my plate and linning. You ho me a milk and butter bill of two 'undred pound, you must 'ave noo laid heggs for your homlets, and cream for your spanil dog' (528).

Now it is made clear to the reader in chapter 37 that the Crawleys take up residence with Raggles immediately on their return from the continent so that by the best reckoning we can make they must have lived in his ''ouse' seven or eight years. So, whereas Thackeray wants to maximise the London period in order to stress the extent of Becky's treachery to Rawdon, we see that he wants to minimise it to make her debts credible (it would be incredible that she could have lived on 'nothing a year' for eight years, even with creditors as trusting as Raggles). In the structurally loose and chronologically vague organisation of the latter part of the novel double dealing of this kind can pass unnoticed. This chronological double dealing also makes believable lecherous Lord Steyne's withholding some eight years (and paying over £1000) before making a serious attempt on Becky's virtue.[28] Answering from impressions rather than calculation most readers would, I think, say that Steyne's connection with the Crawleys lasts some two or three years rather than the best part of a decade.

The fact that all the events are on a sliding time scale means that characters can age or be preserved according to the demands of the immediate scene. Little Rawdon, for example, is described as 'about eight years old' (431) when he eavesdrops on his mother singing to Steyne and has his ears boxed. But this is set in the period of old Sir Pitt's death when the boy should in fact be six. (One remembers, incidentally, how censorious the narrator is of Becky when she forgets the age of her son.) Clearly Thackeray had a sturdy eight-year-old in mind for this scene and so advanced Rawdon to that age. Rawdon's father is subject to the same kind of alteration. Shortly after the above episode we are told that he 'was now five-and-forty years of age' (473) which, at a generous estimate, means that the 'young dragoon' who won Becky at Queen's Crawley was thirty-five years old. But, of course, he was not. Thackeray has for the nonce made Rawdon middle-aged in order to convey an effect of time passed. So also with *his* father. When old Sir Pitt is visited by his newly married son and heir he confides that 'I'm not very fur from fowr-score—he, he' (388). And this was the man who told Becky in proposing six or seven years before 'I'm good for twenty years' (142) and who is shown in the illustrations to the second number as a hale man apparently in his fifties.

In the second half of the novel Thackeray has learned and is applying the lesson that imprecision about dates allows him to organise his material to its most powerful effect and to range at will over impressively long stretches of narrative history. It means that he can survey a whole period, such as Amelia's unhappy years at Fulham, without the irksome need to synchronise events with each other or place them in order. It also means that he can, without strain or artifice, concentrate or expatiate as he wants: the three years between Dobbin's return from India and the continental expedition are digested into less than fifty pages, the subsequent few months at Pumpernickel stretched to nearly seventy. There is a price which has to be paid for this freedom. Thackeray's indefiniteness about chronology encourages the reader to be lazy and unalert in this second half of the novel. A notorious example of this effect are the nonsensically transposed paragraphs in chapter 59 which went uncorrected, and apparently unnoticed for a century.[29] But on the whole the gain in narrative liberty and ease outweighs the loss in definition. The large hazy expanses of the second half of the novel suit Thackeray's genius better than the clear but smaller scale of the first and it is characteristic of the novelist's empirical methods that this success should have been achieved not by more but by less strenuous time-keeping.

2

PENDENNIS

The Two Thackerays and the Limits of Autobiographical Fiction

In his second full length novel Thackeray hit what Trollope would call his 'groove'. *Pendennis* establishes not just the shape of one work but the mould for all the subsequent long fiction Thackeray was to write—the career of a hero (correspondent with his younger self) regarded by a friendly 'biographer' (correspondent with his older self) as he tries and errs his way through the world, gaining a moral education and a wife on the way. This prototype Thackerayan novel, concerned as it is with social *rites de passage*, is less patterned and more inclusive than *Vanity Fair*. It is sententious and dominated by an 'authorial I' who seems more frankly authorial than any previously sustained in his fiction. And as the manner is increasingly confidential so the matter is increasingly auto-biographical. On coming across *Pendennis* in later life the novelist was heard to muse: 'Yes, it is very like—it is certainly very like.'[1] But how like? and what rules did the fastidious Thackeray devise for this kind of fiction where, as Warrington would say, his feelings are sold for money? We find the answers in chapter 41, 'Contains a Novel Incident'. The novel incident is a 'philosophical conversation' (417) between author Pen and critic Warrington about whether or not to publish the auto-biographical *Leaves from the Lifebook of Walter Lorraine*. Since Walter Lorraine is to Pen what Pen is to Thackeray the discussion is, in fact, of more than passing interest. Perhaps it was for the novelist as well: this chapter seems to have been the only sizeable portion of the *Pendennis* manuscript he kept and some corrections, given here, suggest that he was actively debating the question of autobiographical fiction with himself as he wrote. Warrington and Pendennis are really Thackeray himself in two minds. The chapter then, taken together with its manuscript corrections, is both a fascinating example of Thackeray's extemporary methods and of long-term significance for the frankness, or otherwise, of his subsequent fiction.

Pen and Warrington's discussion takes place in the unromantic surroundings of Lamb Court over their bachelors' breakfast. *Walter Lorraine* has been only fleetingly mentioned in the previous narrative and the chapter opens with a fuller account of it:

Mr. Pen during his residence at home, after his defeat at Oxbridge, had occupied himself with various literary compositions, and amongst other | THI | works had | COMPOSED | ⟨written⟩ the greater part of a novel. This book written under the influence of his youthful | DISAPPOINTMENTS ⟨DIFFICULTIES⟩ | ⟨⟨embarrassments⟩⟩ amatory and pecuniary, was of a very fierce gloomy and passionate sort—the Byronic despair, the Wertherian despondency, the mocking bitterness of | FAU | Mephistopheles of Faust, were all reproduced ⟨and developed⟩ in the character of the hero; for our youth had just been learning the German language, and imitated, as almost all clever lads do, his favorite poets and writers. Passages in the volumes once so loved and now read so seldom, | MAY ⟨WERE⟩ | ⟨⟨still bear the⟩⟩ mark | ED WITH | ⟨of⟩ the pencil with which he | SCORED | ⟨noted⟩ them in | OLD | ⟨those | EARLY | ⟩ days. Tears fell upon the leaf ⟨of the book⟩ perhaps, | AND | ⟨or⟩ blistered ⟨the pages of⟩ his manuscript as the passionate young man dashed his thoughts down. | HE REMEM | ⟨If he took⟩ up the book | IN AFTER times | ⟨afterwards⟩ he had no ability or wish to sprinkle the leaves with that early dew | WHICH HIS | of former times: his pencil was no longer eager to score ⟨its⟩ marks of approval: but as he looked over the pages of his manuscript he remembered what had been the over-flowing feelings which had caused him to blot it, and the pain which had inspired the line. If the secret history of books could be written, and the author's private thoughts and meanings noted down along-side of his story, |what| how many |DULL TALES| ⟨insipid volumes⟩ would become interesting and dull tales excite the reader! |PEN THOUGHT| ⟨Many a⟩ bitter smile passed over Pen's face as he read his novel, and he recalled the time and feelings which gave it birth. How pompous some of the |FAVOURITE ⟨BEST⟩| ⟨⟨grand⟩⟩ passages appeared; and how weak others were ⟨in which he thought he had expressed |HIMSELF |his full heart⟩.[2]

One notes how Thackeray controls a natural nostalgic sentimentality by disciplining his expression: the lofty 'composed' gives way to the work-a-day 'written': the romantic turn of phrase 'he remembered . . . in after times' is expunged. The styptically sarcastic 'grand' replaces the paternally approving 'favourite' and 'best'. There is no doubt that in all this Thackeray is thinking of himself and correcting his own responses. One of the scrapbooks he kept while visiting Weimar as a youth has survived and is full of just such extravagantly romantic effusions in prose and poetry as are here credited to Pen. One poem, which surely could have been scrawled by Pen in his Byronic midnight moods at Fairoaks, will suffice to show the quality of this juvenilia:

> then flow flow
> O'er my grief furrowed cheeks, ye burning tears
> Mourn for cold hearts once wont with love to glow
> Mourn for bright hopes departed, wasted years
> My life is
> A frozen winter which expects no springs.[3]

(Thackeray was all of twenty when he copied this tragic sentiment.)

Pen goes on to abuse his novel, but in his heart thinks well of it. Warrington joins him with sincere abuse, satirically reading out one of *Lorraine's* purpler passages. The extract he chooses to guy wounds Pen, however, for it is a covert declaration of the author's (then) undying love for the 'Fotheringay'. *Lorraine* was created as a journal of the heart, the fictional equivalent of Blanche's *Mes Larmes*. This sets Warrington off on his next tirade about authors hawking their emotions for sale:

'Thats the way of poets' said Warrington. 'They fall in love and jilt or are jilted they suffer and they cry out that they suffer more than any other mortals; and when they have experienced feelings enough they note them down in a book and take the book to market. All poets are humbugs, all literary men are humbugs, directly a man begins to sell his feelings for money he's a humbug. It a poet gets a pain in his side from too good a dinner he bellows ai ai louder than Prometheus.'[4]

The context makes it clear that it is the literary profession generally, not just poets, which is primarily aimed at. Warrington's point, and as we shall see it is particularly germane to him, is that it is 'indecent' to publicise one's secret life for money.

The discussion is now warm. Shakespeare, Pen objects, wrote for the market place. The artist, he asserts, reveals his inner feelings because they are finer: 'he sees and feels more keenly: it is that which makes him speak of what he feels and sees' (520). The counter attack is powerful, nonetheless Warrington persists: 'all literary men are humbugs'; the true gentleman is taciturn and keeps his private life private.

Remembering that *Pendennis* is itself an autobiographical novel the argument about the ethics of autobiographical writing has reached an illuminating stage. More so as the plot of *Lorraine* is the plot of the first half of *Pendennis*: what is sauce for Pen must surely also be sauce for Thackeray. There is a distinct authorial self-consciousness in a passage like the following:

There was not the slightest doubt ⟨then⟩ that this document |THEN| contained a great deal of Pen's personal experiences, and that *The Leaves from the Lifebook of Walter Lorraine* would never have been written but for Arthur Pendennis's own private griefs passions and follies. As we have |BEEN MADE| ⟨become⟩ acquainted with these in the first volume of his |HISTORY| ⟨biography⟩ it will not be necessary to make large extracts from the ⟨novel of *Walter Lorraine* in which⟩ the young gentleman had depicted such of them as he thought were |FIT FOR THE PURPOSES OF LITERARY COMPOSITION ⟨HIS STORY⟩ AND ⟨THE WHICH⟩ HAVING NOW A ⟨CERTAIN⟩ STATUS IN THE WORLD OF LETTERS ⟨LITERARY PROFESSION⟩ AND SOME KNOWLEDGE OF PUBLISHERS HE BETHOUGHT HIM THAT HE WOULD GIVE TO THE WORLD| likely to interest the reader, or were suitable for the purposes of his story.[5]

Thackeray is treading very carefully here, conscious of the risk of saying too much in the effort to clarify his views. In the erased line of thought he found himself talking too transparently of himself (Pen as an anonymous hack reviewer of some months' standing has, of course, no 'status in the world of letters'). Hence the deletion and the lame ending to the paragraph.

Gradually the scene is emerging as a dramatisation of a novelist's uncertainty about whether or not to publish parts of his private life. How can one go into print without becoming Warrington's 'humbug'? Pen's argument for doing so now takes on a more aggressive tone, truculent almost in its forced modesty:

Now Pen had never any notion, even in the time of his youthful |HEAT| ⟨inexperience⟩ and fervour of imagination, that the story he was |COMPOSING| ⟨writing⟩ was a masterpiece of composition, |FOR THE| ⟨or that⟩ he was the equal of the great writers whom he admired; and when he ⟨now⟩ reviewed his little performance, he was keenly enough alive to its faults, and pretty modest regarding its merits. It |IS| ⟨was not very⟩ good he thought, but it was |BETTER THAN| ⟨as good as⟩ most books of the kind, that had the run of the circulating libraries and the career of the season. He had |WEIGHED A POPULAR| ⟨critically examined more than one fashionable⟩ novel |OR TWO |by |AN| ⟨the⟩ author⟨s⟩ of the day then popular; and he thought that his intellect was as good ⟨as theirs⟩ and that he could write the English language as well as those ladies or gentlemen; and as |HIS EYE| ⟨he now⟩ ran over his early performance, ⟨he was pleased to find here and there⟩ passages exhibiting both fancy and vigour, and traits, if not of genius, of genuine passion and feeling.[6]

The mood has hardened to one of self-justification: why on earth should Pen *not* publish, if others less scrupulous do? Warrington, now cooler, agrees. Indeed 'Bluebeard' goes so far as to praise the novel for its ingenuousness, choosing a suitably manly image to do so: 'There's a certain greenness and freshness in it which I like somehow. The bloom disappears off the face of poetry after you begin to shave. You can't get up that naturalness and artless rosy tint in after-days' (522).

What then, asks Pen finally, should they do with it: throw it in the fire or take it to the literary market place to be bid for by Bacon and Bungay?

'I dont see what is the good of incremation' ⟨Warrington said:⟩ 'though I have a great mind to put him into the fire to punish your atrocious humbug and hypocrisy. Shall I burn him indeed? You have much too great a value for him to hurt a hair of his head.'

'Have I? Here goes' said Pen and Walter Lorraine went off the table and was flung on to the coals. But the fire |WAS LOW, AND WARRINGTON TAKING UP THE TONGS WITH SOME EAGERNESS RESCUED THE MANUSCRIPT FROM ITS THREATENED DOOM| ⟨having done its duty of boiling the young man's breakfast kettle |WAS| had given up work for the day |AND AS PEN KNEW| and had gone out as Pen knew very well; and Warrington⟩ with a scornful smile once more took up the manuscript with the tongs from out of the |BURNT| harmless cinders.[7]

Again we see Thackeray deliberately stiffening the episode with a dose of satire. Pen's genuinely sacrificial gesture is converted into sham histrionics: Warrington's genuine eagerness into *blasé* languor.[8] After the rescue the older man concludes with some rough praise and a grudging *imprimatur*:

'The rubbish is saleable enough Sir; and my advice to you is this: the next time you go home for a holyday, take Walter Lorraine in your carpet bag—give him a more modern air: prune away, though sparingly, some of the green passages, and add a little comedy and cheerfulness and satire and that sort of thing—and then we'll take him to market and sell him. The book is not a wonder of wonders but it will do very well.'

'Do you think so Warrington' said Pen delighted for this was great praise from his cynical friend.

'You silly young fool I think its uncommonly clever' Warrington said in a kind voice|AND HELD OUT HIS HAND TO THE YOUNG MAN AND| ⟨'So do you Sir.' And|HE TOOK UP| ⟨⟨with⟩⟩ the manuscript⟩ which he held in his hand he playfully struck Pen on the cheek.[9]

To the end Thackeray maintains by correction the satirical severity of Pen's *alter ego*: the comradely handshake becomes a mocking tap.

The whole of this interesting scene may be taken as a critical parable. As J. Y. T. Greig points out Warrington and Pen are self-portraits of the artist as a young man and as a not so young man.[10] Exteriorised in chapter 41 is the creator's dilemma: naïve Pen representing the force of idealistic expression, cynical Warrington that of prudent suppression. The result of the conflict is a compromise. *Lorraine* will be clipped, soured with satire, made less a *roman à clef* (its authorship is kept a secret), lightened by comedy, corrected by the jaundiced eye of after-life—*edited* in a word.

We have then the formula for a limited mode of fiction in which the prime considerations are that it should spring from the author's own deeply felt experience yet be decently re-strained from any improper revelation. There is a striking example of what this means, practically, in the crisis of the novel, Helen Pendennis's death. As she slips away it seems inevitable that mother and son will part forever unreconciled. Suddenly in the twilight Warrington speaks: 'Will you let me tell you something about myself, my kind friends?' What he will tell them at this eleventh hour is the reason why he lives the life of a celibate recluse. He is, it emerges, disastrously married:

'My fate is such as I made it, and not lucky for me or for others involved in it.

'I, too, had an adventure before I went to college; and there was no one to save me as Major Pendennis saved Pen. Pardon me, Miss Laura, if I tell this story before you. It is as well that you all of you should hear my confession. Before I went to college, as a boy of eighteen, I was at a private tutor's, and there, like Arthur, I became attached, or fancied I was attached, to a woman of a much lower degree and a greater age than my own . . . What could come of such a marriage? I found, before long, that I was married to a boor. She could not comprehend one subject that interested me. Her dull-ness palled upon me till I grew to loathe it. And after some time of a wretched, furtive union—I must tell you all—I found letters some-where (and such letters they were!) which showed me that her heart, such as it was, had never been mine, but had always belonged to a person of her own degree.

'At my father's death, I paid what debts I had contracted at college, and settled every shilling which remained to me in an annuity, upon—upon those who bore my name, on condition that they should hide themselves away, and not assume it. They have kept that condition, as they would break it, for more money. If I had earned fame or reputation, that woman would have come to claim it ... and I entered life at twenty, God help me—hopeless and ruined beyond remission. I was the boyish victim of vulgar cheats, and, perhaps, it is only of late I have found out how hard—ah, how hard—it is to forgive them. I told you the moral before, Pen; and now I have told you the fable. Beware how you marry out of your degree' (733–5).

Bluebeard voluntarily opens his secret room to show the wife locked away. He reveals the fable for its moral: it is, by his standards, morally right to tell the story of his inner life to this intimate group in these extreme circumstances. It would, by the same standards, be morally wrong to publicise his inner life for sympathy or literary gain—'directly a man begins to sell his feelings for money he's a humbug'.

Warrington is an influential figure in *Pendennis*, in his conduct and counsel he expresses many of the attitudes which Thackeray brought to the novel as he wrote it. It is not hard in this particular context, to fit Warrington's stoic muteness to the larger situation. *Pendennis* is, to some extent, a confessional work: the hero's story is 'very like' Thackeray's misspent youth (as he chose to represent it), his wasted university career and his beginnings in the literary profession. So much private life may be opened up in the interest of providing instructional and saleable comic fiction. But Thackeray as well as having in his past an idle young manhood like Pendennis's also had a wife locked away like Warrington's,[11] and no less than that Bluebeard was doomed to exile from complete domestic bliss. A line is drawn between what is legitimately within the province of fiction and what is outside its borders. The very deepest experiences of the author's life, if we are to believe what is implied by Warrington's taciturnity, are deemed outside, unmentionable.

53

'Warrington's the man,' wrote one clamorous reviewer demanding more of Bluebeard's story.[12] One agrees: Warrington–Thackeray's 'Fortunes and Misfortunes' would have made a greater novel than Pendennis–Thackeray's. But the novelist was not prepared to sell his deepest feelings for a shilling a month on the bookstalls of London and we never learn anything more about Bluebeard's past than that he has a past. Standing as far away from Thackeray as we do the reticence can be seen as a kind of failure. What posterity has come to admire as Dickens's greatness, for example, is just his ability to render the traumatic experiences of his life into fiction: the blacking factory and the ill-assorted marriage are not withheld in *David Copperfield*. In Thackeray's autobiographical fiction we are always tantalised by the unopened skeleton closet, Bluebeard's locked chamber, what Gordon Ray has called the 'buried life'. The 'secret history' (518) of *Pendennis* stays a secret.

II

Pendennis can be seen to fence the perimeters beyond which the novelist will not go. In large part this self-restraint goes together in Thackeray's mind with a nagging distrust of his medium—the feeling that the novel could not, or should not, express the deepest, most private experiences of a man's life. This distrust is given its most graphic demonstration in *The Virginians* where George Warrington's startling confession that his married life, the story's 'happy ending', has been a sham is cut short with the explanation: 'Here three pages are torn out of Sir George Warrington's MS. book, for which the Editor is sincerely sorry' (905). The three missing pages are, like Bluebeard Warrington's marriage, an unwritten and for Thackeray an unwriteable novel.

Self-restraint in Thackeray's later fiction takes on a physical shape. Like *The Virginians*, *Pendennis* has a shadowy 'editor' who is mentioned once or twice: 'all this narrative,' he says on one occasion, 'is taken from Pen's own confessions' (234). In the subsequent novels the Thackerayan editor working from biographical sources solidifies more clearly as the *moi qui vous parle*. It is a cumbersome way of telling a story which necessitates a lot of explanation as to how certain confidential information was come by.[13] Geoffrey Tillotson, who is one of the few to consider this puzzling aspect of Thackeray's later method, sees the editorial narrator (in this case Pendennis himself in *The Newcomes* and *Philip*) as a half-way stop between personal and impersonal address:

Thackeray's fear at bottom was a fear of being dragged as a person into practical affairs. To make Pendennis the fictional narrator of Thackeray's fiction was a means of retreating into what the most earnest or the least literary readers must see as nearer to inaccessibility. On the other hand he knew he must not retreat too far.[14]

This is true and Tillotson deserves great credit for being the first to make the observation. One would, however, add a rider: Thackeray's fear at bottom was also a fear of being dragged as a person into *personal* affairs. With his other functions the editor acts as a kind of Freudian censor, ensuring that the inner life stays forever inner.

3

HENRY ESMOND
The Virtues of Carelessness

There are two quite contradictory accounts of the composition of *Esmond* and the care that went into it. According to Gordon Ray, 'that the novel is Thackeray's most careful and consummate work of art may be taken as established'. It is this care Ray tells us, which makes *Esmond* so different from the run of Thackeray's fiction—almost un-Thackerayan, in fact:

The monthly parts of *Vanity Fair* and *Pendennis* were customarily dashed off a few days before they were to be published, the printer's boy sometimes waiting in the hall at Young Street to carry off his sheets as they were finished. *Esmond,* on the other hand, was planned as a unit, written deliberately and at leisure, and elaborately revised before any part of it was set up in type.[1]

This statement supports the received opinion that *Esmond* is to be set respectably apart from the slapdash serial novels. 'That careless disrespect,' wrote Lewes reviewing the novel in the *Leader*, 'is nowhere visible in *Esmond.* If as a work of art *Esmond* has defects, they are not the defects of carelessness.'[2] And predictably Trollope lauds the novel because it is, as he judges 'his only work . . . in which there is no touch of idleness' (124). Praise indeed!

A less popular tradition, although ultimately as authoritative, suggests that the book had a much easier delivery. It can be traced through Leslie Stephen writing to Trinity College, Cambridge, to whom he donated the manuscript. Stephen cited the novelist's daughter as telling him that 'there was no previous copy. Thackeray wrote (or dictated) the manuscript as it stands without previously putting anything on paper, and it was sent in this form to the printers.' And elsewhere in the same correspondence Stephen writes:

Mrs. Ritchie tells me, he dictated it without having previously written anything. The copy was sent straight to press as it stands, with, as you will see, remarkably little alteration. As *Esmond* is generally considered to be his most perfect work in point of style, I think that this is a remarkable fact and adds considerably to the interest of the MS.[3]

Stephen is supported in this by Eyre Crowe who when he joined Thackeray as his amanuensis observed that the first part of *Esmond* had been written 'with scarcely any interpolations or marginal *repentirs*'.[4] As for 'leisure' Elwin rightly notes that Thackeray undertook to write *Esmond* during an extraordinarily hectic period of his life and in consequence 'failed to finish the book till several months after the prescribed date'.[5] And as regards internal structure Greig, for one, has criticised Thackeray's failure to lay the ground in the early sections for the later developments of *Esmond's* plot.[6]

The controversy here may be reduced to one on working methods. *Esmond* is unique among Thackeray's major novels in that it was written entirely before publication. Did the novelist, as is commonly believed, substantially change his mode of composition for this novel, or was it thrown off in the same improvisatory way as *Vanity Fair* and the rest? Does it really deserve the description Thackeray applied to it in later life, his 'careful book'?[7]

For the general reader *Esmond* has always presented the aspect of an intricate and carefully mounted work, one which is distanced by anachronistic style and stiffened by historical research. Two structural features confirm this impression:

the complicated balances and conflicts of Harry's love life and, more formally, the way in which the novel is circumscribed by its own narrative technique—Esmond, Sen. (ca. 1745) recounting the career of Esmond, Jun. (ca. 1700), edited by the aggressive Rachel Esmond Warrington (ca. 1780), with annotation by three generations of the Esmond family, the whole encased in what is basically the plot of the unwritten *Virginians*. Without denying or detracting from the novel's manifest complexity, it is my aim to show that Thackeray arrived at it less by lengthy foreplanning and revision than by almost accidental discovery and rapid adaptations as he went along, the final shape emerging in his mind only when he was well on the way to finishing. I shall attempt to prove that *Esmond*, in fact, is genetically no different from the novels published from month to month in numbers and that one of its most perplexing aspects—the 'incestuous' overtones of the Harry–Rachel relationship[8]—arises from Thackeray's *not* revising early work in the light of its later evolution. The main point I shall be driving at is that, far from revising the novel carefully, Thackeray was prepared to make great creative efforts so as not to have to rewrite anything.

II

Perhaps the most frequently quoted judgement on *Esmond* is George Eliot's casual comment: 'The most uncomfortable book you can imagine . . . The hero is in love with the daughter all through the book and marries the mother at the end.'[9] George Eliot did not, of course, intend this arch comment from a letter to stand as a public verdict. But even so, the inference that *Esmond*'s ending is unprepared-for is grossly insensitive. That there is something more than filial chivalry between the lady and her knight, and possibly between the lady and her page, is evident to the attentive reader well before the close. George Eliot must have been skipping to have overlooked, for example, the groundwork in the description of Esmond's play, the *Faithful Fool*:

A young woman was represented with a great number of suitors, selecting a pert fribble of a peer, in place of the hero (but ill-acted, I think, by Mr. Wilks, the Faithful Fool), who persisted in admiring her. In the fifth act Teraminta was made to discover the merits of Eugenio (the F.F.), and to feel a partiality for him too late; for he announced that he had bestowed his hand and estate upon Rosaria, a country lass, endowed with every virtue. (343)

Clearly, Teraminta is Beatrix, Eugenio is Esmond (well born indeed if she but knew it) and Rosaria is Rachel—the 'countrified' widow, as she is called, who once remembered that Harry liked roses. Clearly, too, this forecasts the end of the novel, which must have been firmly in Thackeray's mind at this point. How far back can one carry the forecast? And was the ending in Thackeray's mind when he started to write? Those who, with Ray, maintain that the novel was 'planned as a unit' would say that it was, and that the first clear hint of the way things are to develop is probably Rachel's unreasonable jealousy at Harry's calf-love for Nancy Sievewright, the blacksmith's daughter.[10]

There is, however, a major deletion in the manuscript of *Esmond* which suggests that prevision of the Rachel–Harry union was not there from the first, that originally Thackeray began to write a novel with a much simpler love plot and simpler time scheme, and that the first book of *Esmond* belongs to this simpler novel. The passage has been dropped from the account of Steele's visit to Harry while he is in prison suffering from his wounds and from Rachel's cruel reproaches for his part in the duel. The piece would have come at the end of the sentimental captain's speech which, in the published text, ends

59

abruptly (as does his visit) with an enthusiastic tribute to Rachel: 'I thought her even more noble than the virgin' (181). In the manuscript there follows this reflection, crossed out but still legible:

When Harry's kind Ambassador left him the young man sate lost in the thought—the selfish thought which occupied him. There is many a feeling in the heart which a man is ashamed to confess to himself even. And Mr. Esmond had one or two such in his—unacknowledged but present—not recognized but cherished, as a woman goes and nurses a secret child.

From the day when as a child he first beheld her, and almost until he went to college, this lad had devoted his boyish adoration to my lady Viscountess, thought the whole world contained no being so perfect; hung upon her looks, ran at her bidding and prevented all her wants; and thought a smile or a permission to kiss her hand was the richest reward life could offer him. After two years of Cambridge and such a life as students had there, this harmless childish flame passed away—the young man preserving his love for his dear mistress still, but driven by the natural impulse which *genus omne animantium*[11] obeys, and which sends the youth from the fondest mother's apron strings, and the girl from the best beloved father's side when the time comes.

Beatrice had been growing to that perfection of beauty which all who have known her have admired in her; and in the last year of Mr. Esmond's life at College, and especially on that last day when he parted with her when he was about to make the fatal journey to London with my Lord Viscount, he found to what a pitch his passion had grown for the most lovely creature eyes ever looked on. 'Twas of her Esmond thought as they lay on the road, sending his soul after her back again to Castlewood, blessing her name, as he lay awake thinking of her, enjoying the very stars and moon because they could shine into her chamber.

If nothing else, this shows how elastic future details of the plot were for Thackeray as he wrote. In the novel as it continues, Esmond does not fall in love with the mature Beatrix until years later, after he has won his spurs at Vigo. I shall return to this, but we may draw some immediate conclusions from the passage. Nowhere in the published work is there anything which juxtaposes as clearly and comparatively Esmond's feelings for the two love objects in his life. And certainly there is no suggestion that Esmond *transfers* his passion from one to the other. Rather, by deliberate haziness, Thackeray manages to imply that Esmond is deeply in love with both at once. It is not a case of oscillation so much as emotional ambiguity. Hence, such contrived equivocation with the term 'mistress' as this from the opening of the third book:

Truly a ludicrous and pitiable object [was Esmond], at least exhausting everybody's pity but his dearest mistress's, Lady Castlewood's, in whose tender breast he reposed all his dreary confessions, and who never tired of hearing him and pleading for him.

Sometimes Esmond would think there was hope. Then again he would be plagued with despair, at some impertinence or coquetry of his mistress [i.e. Beatrix]. (340)

The clear, unequivocal, and discarded analysis of Esmond's feelings in prison, however, would seem to indicate a different plan in which the adult hero was henceforth to be single-mindedly in love with Beatrix (or 'Beatrice' as she then was). It is hard to see how Thackeray could have fanned the 'boyish adoration . . . the harmless childish flame' back to life or entangled Esmond once more in his 'fondest mother's apron strings' without making him seem a milksop. Underlying the deleted passage, and presumably what went before, seems to be a pattern more like that of Thackeray's previous novel *Pendennis*. Rachel was, like Helen Pendennis, to suffer a 'sexual pang' (although examined more courageously) at being superseded by her daughter (or foster daughter as Laura Bell was) in her son's affections (or foster son as Harry was). Thus, the Rachel–Esmond–Beatrix triangle was to be congruent with the Helen–Pen–Laura triangle rather than, as it more interestingly becomes, with Scott's Rebecca–Ivanhoe–Rowena. And the graduation into adult life and sex was for Harry, as for Pen, to come after mild debauchery at Cambridge. Grown up, Harry, like Arthur, was to put his childish attachments away.

There is some corroborative evidence for this interpretation. One of Thackeray's finer strokes in the novel was his naming the heroine Rachel. It keeps alive an expectation of the ending by its faint biblical allusion to the long deferred marriage of Jacob and Rachel. That it was meant to have this function is clear from an exchange between Harry and Beatrix (again in the third book) in which he assures her of his steadfast love and she whimsically replies with a pun on names:

'How long was it that Jacob served an apprenticeship for Rachel?'

'For mamma?' says Beatrix. 'Is it mamma your honour wants, and that I should have the happiness of calling you papa?'

Esmond blushed again. (357)

But Thackeray did not hit on Rachel's premonitory Christian name until the novel was well advanced, to just past the prison scenes, in fact. Before this Rachel Castlewood was, less felicitously, Dolly Castlewood. It is tempting to think that Thackeray renamed her (going back as he did to cross out 'Dolly' where it had occurred) in accordance with his new vision of the novel's development. At about the same time he changed 'Beatrice' to 'Beatrix' for perhaps the same reason— the Dantean evocation of unshakable devotion being less appropriate than the neutral fact that the girl was named, as we are later told, after James II's queen in whose reign she was born.

The argument is, of course, more speculative than one would

like. But if it is accepted a number of previous anomalies are cleared up. Thackeray's removing Rachel–Dolly's looks in the first hundred pages is an example. Her beauty, we are told, 'was very much injured' by the smallpox which Harry brought to Castlewood:

> When the marks of the disease cleared away, they did not, it is true, leave furrows or scars on her face (except one, perhaps, on her forehead over her left eyebrow); but the delicacy of her rosy colour and complexion were gone: her eyes had lost their brilliancy, her hair fell, and her face looked older. It was as if a coarse hand had rubbed off the delicate tints of that sweet picture, and brought it, as one has seen unskilful painting-cleaners do, to the dead colour. Also, it must be owned, that for a year or two after the malady, her ladyship's nose was swollen and redder. (88)

Handicapped by these ravages, how does she contrive, eighteen years later, to look younger than her blossoming daughter? The answer may well be that at that early stage Thackeray had not intended to preserve her for a marriage late in life—that the whole love plot was still fluidly alterable in his mind.

III

There were other reasons for being dissatisfied with the arrangement of having Esmond's change of allegiance take place in prison. These also bear witness to the flexibility of Thackeray's plans as he wrote the novel, his reluctance to go back and rewrite, his habit of taking major changes from one page to the next and, not least, the carelessness which often forced these changes. In chapter 11 of the first book Thackeray had become tangled up with his time settings. Careful readers of this part of the novel will notice that there is doubt, even contradiction, about when Holt visited Castlewood with the news of Harry's legitimate birth (1696 or 1700?),[12] and about when Mohun entered the Castlewoods' circle. Another chronological error was the failure to bring Beatrix on to puberty. Five months before her father's death we find her prattling on Esmond's knee (115), and the end of chapter 12 confirms that she is thirteen years old at the time. If, therefore, it was 'in the last year of Mr. Esmond's life at College' that 'he found to what a pitch his passion had grown for the most lovely creature eyes ever looked upon,' he, a twenty-one-year-old man, must have been in love with a Beatrix of twelve, Lolita's age.

Clearly this would not do. The easiest remedy would have been to go back and revise a little. Instead, almost without breaking his stride, Thackeray reconstructs his scheme for the next section of his novel, and a very interesting reconstruction it is. First Esmond has to be occupied until Beatrix can advance to respectable sexual attractions. On his release from prison he is therefore sent off to Vigo on one of the early skirmishes of the War of Spanish Succession. This, with some judicious narrative acceleration, gives Beatrix a necessary three years in which to attain 'the perfection of her beauty'. And meanwhile Thackeray had decided to complicate the circumstances of his hero's falling in love with her by completely reconstituting him emotionally. On his return from the Vigo expedition Harry is told by his new patroness, the dowager countess, that young Tusher is making love to Rachel. This arouses in him a 'strange and sudden excitement' (207). Defying his banishment he hurries down to Walcote, is reunited with his mistress in Winchester Cathedral, and is almost at once relieved of his jealous fears that she is about to become Mrs Tusher. Thus relieved, he suggests that she should become his own wife. The form of his proposal is delicate but nonetheless obviously a proposal of marriage:

'Why should I ever leave you? If God hath given me this great boon—and near or far from me, as I know now—the heart of my dearest mistress follows me; let me have that blessing near me, nor ever part with it till life separate us. Come away—leave this Europe, this place which has so many sad recollections for you. Begin a new life in a new world. My good lord often talked of visiting that land in Virginia which King Charles gave us—gave his ancestor. Frank will give us that. No man there will ask if there is a blot on my name, or inquire in the woods what my title is. (214)

Rachel declines on grounds of 'duty' but so gently that there is still hope for Esmond. They embrace, then return to the house to be met by Beatrix descending the stairs into the hall. It is Esmond's first sight of Beatrix the woman, and on the spot, with the other woman he has just asked to be his wife by his side, he falls desperately in love with her.

The scene of Beatrix's descent at Walcote is a justly famous one, and it tells us something of Thackeray's genius that it should have come about as a result of his being unable to keep dates straight in his mind and a disinclination to rewrite what was already written. For we may see now how radically and spontaneously he reshaped his novel, or at least those parts which were still in his mind rather than on paper.

Originally Esmond was to have done with Rachel and to have gone on to the *filia pulcrior* as a natural part of the growing-up process. But because Thackeray had neglected to have Beatrix grow up as well, this was impossible. Instead of going back and carefully ageing Beatrix in those scenes where her age appeared, with the instincts of the serial novelist who cannot change what is written and published, he drastically changed his plan of things to come. In so doing Thackeray enriched his novel with what he and most of his readers have felt to be his finest moments. Here, surely, we see the reflexes of the brilliant improviser—the author for whom 'lisping in numbers' was an ineradicable habit of composition. And it does not help us in appreciating his facile improvisation to talk of 'elaborate revision' or 'care'. Thackeray simply crossed out three paragraphs which were going in the wrong direction and in short order invented a brilliantly corrected version of his plot.

IV

The point I have been making, perhaps labouring, is that *Esmond*, in spite of being published in three volumes, is a novel like *Vanity Fair* or *Pendennis* whose virtues as well as vices arise from what Trollope would call the author's idleness. I agree with Leslie Stephen that the remarkable fact is how little —rather than how much—revision we find in the manuscript. The last part of my argument will, I hope, bear out the way in which Thackeray was, until almost the last page of his novel, responsive to new promptings from his imagination—but at the same time reluctant to go back and actually rewrite or fill in what had gone before, even where this would have been as easy as it was desirable.

The most effective counterweight to what Thackeray called *Esmond*'s 'cutthroat melancholy'[13] is the omnipresence in it of Rachel Esmond Warrington, the editor. From the preface onwards, the reader is half-conscious of her comically fussing at the edge of the novel, distancing and balancing the proceedings. This editorial interference, with the retrospection of Harry's own narrative, the family footnotes, and the bridge to *The Virginians*, gives the impression that Thackeray took almost Jamesian pains with the way in which the novel is told. In fact, the full narrative circumstances of *Esmond* did not develop until the work was more than two-thirds through and then from motives that were historical rather than literary.

Apart from the dedication, the preface is the last thing which

Thackeray wrote in *Esmond*. If one did not guess this from its command over all the events of the plot, there is proof in the manuscript. From the evidence of handwriting, paper and ink (there is a good assortment of each), it is quite obvious to the eye that the preface was written continuously from the last page without so much as a break in composition. Logically, then, the preface should have been an appendix. But by advancing it to the head of the work, Thackeray was able to cover up the fact that this elaboration had emerged gradually. It is a simple device but an effective one, and it saves altering the written text. By relegating the preface to the end of the work, where it belongs, we can trace in a straight line the evolution of the narrative apparatus and with it the growing complexity of the novel.

The first footnotes we encounter are on pages 27 and 60. In them Esmond comments on the old viscountess's ambition to have the rank of Marquis and Groom of the Posset restored. The next footnote is given some 150 pages later and is simply a quotation in the original Greek from Homer appropriate to the deserved misfortunes of the Stuarts. This rather Bulwerian embellishment is unsigned but certainly another of Esmond's, the only scholar in the family. The fourth note, initialled 'H.E.', identifies 'the good and faithful lad of Hampshire' (239) who saved his master's life at Blenheim as John Lockwood. This need not be considered here since it is one of the very few additions Thackeray made to his text after it had been sent to the printers. Clearly it is intended to rectify a temporary forgetfulness of Lockwood's name, although it would have been more to Thackeray's credit as a reviser of his work if he had got 'John' Lockwood's name right. Elsewhere he is Tom, Job and Jack.[14]

Up to this point there has been no hint of an editor. The novel is more than half over and Esmond well into his career

as a young officer in Marlborough's campaigns. We know that
Thackeray undertook a great deal of original research for this
phase of the novel, and it is from his scruples as a historian that
the idea of editing the history now arises. Thackeray's picture
of Marlborough is, as has been often noted, very close to
Macaulay's in the first two volumes of *The History of England*
(1848). Thackeray was clearly influenced by his eminent friend
although he had his own reason for disliking Marlborough and
presenting him as a treacherous miser, perversely endowed
with military genius. This reason was the direct kinship which
he acknowledged (fallaciously as it turned out) with John
Richmond Webb. The story of how Webb was slighted by
Marlborough after his victory is familiar to anyone who has
read the novel, and, we are told, the novelist's account of
Wynendael is better than anything done by professional
historians.[15] But Thackeray goes beyond mere chronicling of
the episode into some very murky historical speculations. At
the end of chapter 14, for example, it is alleged that Marlborough was bribed by the French into letting Webb be
ambushed by a vastly superior force of the enemy. This purely
historical allegation is tantamount to accusing the commander-
in-chief of attempted murder as well as high treason. To back
up the preposterous theory (which he claimed in a later letter
to have seriously believed at the time),[16] Thackeray alludes to
how Marlborough 'had betrayed Tollemache at Brest' (286).

Now the Tollemache affair, and the constructions put on it
by Macaulay, came near to discrediting the whole *History*.
The facts were that in 1694 a raid on Brest failed and its com-
mander, Thomas Tollemache, was killed because, it was
suspected, Marlborough had forewarned the French to expect
the attack. This, 'the basest of all the hundred villainies of
Marlborough',[17] was the foundation of Macaulay's calumnious
portraiture and, as his critics soon discovered, a very shaky

foundation, since it could not be proved that Marlborough was in fact solely responsible for this treachery.[18]

Although *Esmond* precedes the public controversy, Thackeray must have had a painful twinge about the distortions to which his adherence to the Whig line was leading him, especially with regard to Marlborough. For at this point in the novel he begins to employ his footnotes to undercut Esmond's extreme views (which in more reckless moments were his own) and less timidly to provide evidence for these views. And in so doing he accidentally creates the editorial machinery which transforms the novel. The first of these dissenting notes, on page 243, is appended to Esmond's comment: 'Should any child of mine take the pains to read these, his ancestor's memoirs, I would not have him judge of the great duke by what a contemporary has written of him.' The note to this runs: 'This passage in the memoirs of Esmond is written on a leaf inserted into the Ms. book, and dated 1744, probably after he had heard of the duchess's death.' This anonymous observation is the first appearance of any second voice in the narrative and a transitional point in the development of Esmond's autobiography into Esmond's family-edited private papers. Structurally it is an important moment, although, as I say, structure was not Thackeray's main preoccupation here. He was more concerned in hedging his historical bets by separating his opinions from those of his hero, making Harry appear emotionally partisan and unreliable—hence the disclaimer and the invented editor to make clear that it is a recantation made by Esmond in the wisdom of his later years.

The next footnote, fifty pages on, confirms that uneasiness about his historical assumptions was forcing Thackeray into traducing his hero. Again it concerns the duke, and picks up one of Esmond's wilder accusations about bribery at Lille. This is qualified by comment from the hero's grandchildren (the 'any child of mine' idea has taken firm root), who cite evidence heard from their grandmother that Harry was hopelessly prejudiced against the great man ever since 'on his first presentation to my lord duke, the duke turned his back upon my grandfather; and said to the duchess, who told my lady dowager at Chelsea, who afterwards told Colonel Esmond: "Tom Esmond's bastard has been to my levee: he has the hangdog look of his rogue of a father"' (293).

We see at this point just how much the instincts of the prudential historian are at variance with the novelist. Harry, we are told, is not to be trusted. The man whom Rachel thinks good enough to be a saint, Frank regards as a king, and Beatrix considers the true head of the Esmond family is here represented as a spiteful bigot who would malign a great contemporary to revenge a snub. That Thackeray is responding to purely local pressures and worries is evident if we look back to chapter 5 of the second book where a flatly contradictory description of Marlborough's reception of Esmond at this levee is given:

That great man received the young one with very especial favour, so Esmond's comrades said, and deigned to say that he had received the best reports of Mr. Esmond, both for courage and ability, whereon you may be sure the young gentleman made a profound bow, and expressed himself eager to serve under the most distinguished captain in the world. (203)

We may note, as another nail into the careful revision theory, that on the evidence of the preface the Warrington twins were one year old at the time of their grandmother Rachel's death. So if 'our grandmother used to tell us children' about Marlborough's insult, she was talking to singularly unheeding or singularly precocious ears.

This note, a longish one, finishes with 'We have General

Webb's portrait now at Castlewood, Va.' It was, however, to have been even longer. The manuscript continues with 'fifteen years after Colonel Esmond's death Macpherson's original papers were published which contain proof of Mr. Esmond's opinions concerning Marlborough'. James Macpherson's *Original Papers; Containing the Secret History of Great Britain from the Restoration to the Accession of the House of Hanover* was one of the historical source books used extensively and sometimes indiscriminately in the preparation for *Esmond* (the fact that it was published in 1775 explains the necessity for bringing in grandchildren rather than immediate descendants). This postscript from the 'original papers' was bitten off not because Thackeray wished to remove it as dubious and irrelevant but, on the contrary, because he intended to expand it, vastly. A little later, at the end of the 'historical' second book, he planned to introduce what was virtually a historical apologia, a huge footnote extending over two or three pages. At the close of this book in the manuscript we find this instruction to the printers: 'Note to the end of chapter XIV . . . This note should be made to go over three pages or else be included in one—otherwise the headings will have to be altered.' The note itself is introduced (in Thackeray's hand):

My grandfather's bad opinion of the famous Marlborough, if not confirmed, at least is borne out by the following extract from Carte's memorandum book in Mr. Macpherson's 'Original Papers' containing the secret history of Great Britain published at London last year (1775).

There then follows (in his secretary's handwriting) the long, turgid and gossipy account by Carte saying that Marlborough might have been open to bribes over the Lille business. It is, to put it charitably, out of place in a novel, however historical.

Fortunately the novelist had the good sense to withdraw this elephantine intrusion and there is no trace of it in the *Esmond* given to his public. But the scaffolding erected to counter-balance his second-volume picture of Marlborough remained and was now put to other profitable uses in the last third of the novel. Committed to interrupting voices, Thackeray, with obvious enjoyment, created a kind of comic counterpoint in the last section between the narrative and an aged and queru-lous Rachel (see the notes to pp. 298, 299 and 314). This reached a climax in a footnote to Esmond's comment on page 407 that 'I have known a woman preach Jesuit's bark, and afterwards Dr. Berkeley's tar-water, as though to follow them were a divine decree, and to refuse them no better than blas-phemy.' The jibe at Rachel is taken up by the lady herself:

My husband was ever in the habit of sneering at women; but the truth we know will prevail against all wit. Though I have lost my confidence in Jesuit's powder thinking it made our little Rachel ill, yet I have not the slightest doubt that Dr. Rock's pills are amongst the most precious medicines ever discovered and am thankful to them as for all other benefits to mankind. N.B. two of our negroes and the overseer's wife have within the last month benefitted amazingly and proved the efficacy, under Providence, of Dr. Rock's discovery.

After writing this passage, Thackeray deleted it. Nor is it hard to see why, on reflection, he must have felt that the joke had gone too far. Within fifty pages Rachel was to yield with 'eyes of meek surrender' (463) to Harry, and it would be disastrous to superimpose on this tricky scene the image of a crotchety eccentric dosing the plantation slaves. But the notion of a comic Rachel was appealing; so the character was foisted onto the newborn 'little Rachel' (her mother's subsequent two footnotes are respectively neutral and poignant). This lady makes her debut in a brief fact-giving note on page 419 and then as a full-blown character in a note to page 432. This, in the last pages of the novel, is the stepping-stone to the superbly wrought preface with its portrait of the pugnacious Rachel Esmond Warrington, later to become one of Thackeray's finest comic creations.

The track which one follows through the footnotes is, with the help of the manuscript, a clear, progressive and informative one. Originally Esmond himself was to present his story, and the novel continues in this way until well into the second volume. An attempt to distance Esmond–Thackeray's opinions about Marlborough resulted in the creation of an editorial apparatus. This is embellished and worked back into the novel as an elaborate frame in the third volume (but not in the previous two) by turning Esmond's autobiography into family-edited papers.

If the author of *Esmond* were the alleged careful novelist, the track would have been obscured. A careful Thackeray would certainly have gone back and sown his narrative from the early chapters with footnotes and interpolations by R.E.W. and the others. He did not. He did, however, lop off a few outgrowing notes at a later stage, but hardly in such a way as to merit the compliment that he was revising carefully, especially since those notes he left are littered with small errors. What one learns from the extempore inventions which result in the final narrative shape of the novel are lessons which hold good for *Esmond* generally: that it is, like the rest of Thackeray's best fiction, carelessly brilliant. Although the novelist took commendable pains with the historical preparation, *Esmond* was written, like his other novels, at the serialist's creative gallop in which the ground could be covered only once. It is Thackeray the improviser, not Thackeray the reviser, whom we should salute in *Esmond*.

4

THE NEWCOMES
The Well Planned Baggy Monster

For *The Newcomes* we have what must be the prize exhibit among Thackeray's working materials—a forward plan of the last nine numbers, clearly written in advance of any of them:

XVI.   The Colonel comes back, and proposes to Barnes for Ethel for Clive. Rupture between the Colonel and Barnes.

XVII.   Announcement of her engagement to Lord Farintosh, death of Lady Kew.

XVIII.   Clive's marriage. Binnie's Nunc Dimittis.

XIX.   Elopement of Lady Clara. Ethel's revolt.

XX.   The Election. Height of Clive's prosperity. Bitterness at home.

XXI.   Failure of the B.B. Mrs. Mack comes to live with the young people.

XXII.   Retreat of the Colonel before her. His resolve and its execution.

XXIII.IV. Orme's History of India. Too late. The Colonel's Euthenasia.[1]

These notes occupy the top half of a sheet of note paper. Evidently they are continued from a first completed sheet and if Thackeray's handwriting is consistent—which it usually is at this stage of his life—it would mean that plans of a similar kind were made from near the beginning.

In his discussion of *The Newcomes* Gordon Ray comments: 'Thackeray adhered closely to this plan, though certain incidents were deferred for one number.'[2] This is true enough of the sequence of main events, but Ray is slightly misleading in not indicating how bare the plan is. The point may be easiest made by juxtaposing with the above a reader's synopsis of what actually happens in the sixteenth number, the first for which there is an entry in the plan:

Chapter 48: Death of Ethel's father Sir Brian. The accession of Barnes and his *rapprochement* with the other side of the family. Pen's marriage to Laura. Clive's new prosperity with the Bundelcund Banking Company. Jack Belsize's (Lord Highgate's) attentions to the Newcomes' ladies, especially Barnes's wife, Lady Clara. Lord Kew's domestication. The B.B.C.'s vast success.

Chapter 49: A dramatic dialogue between Pen and Laura on the sanctity of marriage. Highgate's suspicious interest in Barnes's wife. Dinner at Hobson Newcome's. The death of Major Pendennis.

Chapter 50: Clive's unhappiness amidst prosperity. J.J.'s success as an artist. Ethel's unhappiness. Pen and Laura's married bliss.

Chapter 51: The Colonel returns. Laura's motherhood. Clive's continuing love for Ethel. The Colonel proposes to Barnes for Ethel for Clive.

Comparison shows how much more is involved than is forecast in the plan. Most of the number, in fact, reveals Thackeray either keeping old narrative irons warm or making room for new ones. Hence the action is distributed among four groups of characters, not one as preconceived. What these notes emerge as, on analysis, is less a synopsis than a series of large and somewhat isolated signposts. Yet one cannot but be impressed with the length of vision which the plan shows. In the sixteenth number, for example, we can see Thackeray laying ground for the nineteenth—'Elopement of Lady Clara'—both directly by hinting at the real motive for Highgate's gallantry and indirectly by long passages devoted to Laura and Pen's matrimonial happiness. The Pendennis exchanges on the sanctity of marriage, which modern readers often find morally unctuous, thus emerge as a cunningly designed counterpoint to the Barnes–Clara wretchedness and the Highgate–Clara recklessness.

This deep planning is not normally a visible feature of Thackeray's fiction. It was not his habit to anticipate later events in his novels, either by direct prediction, structural parallelism or prophetic imagery. In other ways he seems to have been unusually close with this kind of information: his letters rarely give away the future course of his narratives. Even in the plan he made for himself here we can see a certain reticence: take the note for Number XXII 'Retreat of the Colonel before her. His resolve and its execution'—had Thackeray died at XXI it would have been a very wide-awake reader who could have guessed what the old man's 'resolve and ... execution' were to be. Yet there have been hints and with hindsight we can pick them up. Gordon Ray, for example, points out the scene at the beginning of *The Newcomes* where the Colonel (visiting Greyfriars) is described 'Under the great archway ... standing between the shouting boys and the tottering seniors.'[3] This can be remembered by the alert reader as having foretold the hero's final refuge.

In the epilogue to his novel Thackeray made what was, for him, a rather curious assertion about this prevision in *The Newcomes*:

Two years ago, walking with my children in some pleasant fields near to Berne, in Switzerland, I strayed from them into a little wood; and, coming out of it presently, told them how the story had been revealed to me somehow, which for three and twenty months the reader has been pleased to follow. (1007)

The business about the will in Orme's *India* which is set up at the beginning of the novel so as to solve everything at the end probably explains a part of this uncharacteristic boast. Another part is evident from a visit Thackeray made to Charterhouse in early 1855 when he told a boy there 'Colonel Newcome is going to be a Codd' and actually asked to see a likely model among the school's pensioners for his hero *in extremis*.[4]

II

Having come this far the reader who knows *The Newcomes* well will have been struck by a teasing paradox. It is, notoriously, a shapeless work. In fact it was about *The Newcomes* that Henry James coined his much repeated attack on the mid-Victorian novel as a great loose baggy monster.[5] Yet, manifestly, *The Newcomes* is the only novel of which we can confidently say, 'Thackeray planned it.' How is this to be explained? And should we deduce a similar preconceived framework in the other fiction? And how does one square the Berne anecdote with that authorial self-portrait, quoted earlier in the Introduction:

Alexandre Dumas describes himself, when inventing the plan of a work, as lying silent on his back for two whole days on the deck of a yacht in a Mediterranean port. At the end of the two days he arose and called for dinner. In those two days he had built his plot. He had moulded a mighty clay, to be cast presently in perennial brass. The chapters, the characters, the incidents, the combinations were all arranged in the artist's brain ere he set a pen to paper. *My Pegasus won't fly, so as to let me survey the field below me* . . . (xvii, 596)

In answer one should first make the point that novelists devise plans for various reasons and in various circumstances. After an easy opening Thackeray found it more difficult to get on with the *The Newcomes* than any work he had previously undertaken. A terse comment in his diary, commemorating the completion of the twelfth number, records the difficulty graphically: 'I had hoped to have done 24 numbers by this time: but illness changes moving small domestic hindrances have prevented the work.'[6]

It is likely, I would suggest, that Thackeray made the long-term number plan of *The Newcomes* because he was exhausted, depressed and distracted. It served as a crutch to sustain a limping imagination. Just as a man with a failing memory might have to write things down that he could formerly keep in his head or invent on the spur of the moment, so Thackeray was reduced to this ration-card (two incidents per number)[7] approach to *The Newcomes*. It is, I guess, highly improbable that any such written schedule was made for the previous masterpieces—*Vanity Fair*, *Pendennis* and *Esmond*. For them he could rely on an abundant vitality to keep the plot going.

Nor did the blueprint improve the organisation of *The Newcomes*. Take the number we have summarised, XVI. On the page it will be found disproportionate, abrupt in its transitions and badly paced. It starts in chapter 48 with a long, slow, digressive essay on death: towards the end it crams the meat of the number (the Colonel proposing for Ethel) into one short and truncated chapter (51). In the second half of the number Thackeray is so pressed that he cannot allow himself the proper dramatic treatment of scenes which cry out for it. Hence the magnificent Major Pendennis is allowed to perish in a feeble parenthesis on Laura's sanctity:

Not many more feasts was Arthur Pendennis, senior, to have in this world. Not many more great men was he to flatter, nor schemes to wink at, nor earthly pleasures to enjoy. His long days were well nigh ended: on his last couch, which Laura tended so affectionately, with his last breath almost, he faltered out to me, 'I had other views for you, my boy, and once hoped to see you in a higher position in life;

but I begin to think now, Arthur, that I was wrong; and as for that girl, sir, I am sure she is an angel.'

May I not inscribe the words with a grateful heart? Blessed he—blessed though maybe undeserving—who has the love of a good woman. (658)

Thackeray can do much better than this as, for example, the death of Beatrix Bernstein in *The Virginians* will readily show.

To find the best things in *The Newcomes* we must ignore Thackeray's plan-making and look to that area of creative freedom which he always allowed himself. There is a relevant anecdote on the subject told by Lady Ritchie. After writing a portion of *The Newcomes* Thackeray appeared to take tea in the company of a group of young ladies:

The coming number of 'The Newcomes', of course, was in all our minds. Miss Hennell, as our spokeswoman, said 'Mr. Thackeray, we want you to let Clive marry Ethel. Do let them be happy.' He was surprised at our interest in his characters. 'What a fuss you make about my yellow books here in the country! In town no one cares for them. They haven't the time. The characters once created *lead me*, and I follow where they direct. I cannot tell the events that wait on Clive and Ethel.'[8]

If we check with the plan we see that Thackeray indeed left the final Ethel–Clive–Rosey triangle out of his calculations, and most readers will agree with Miss Hennell that it is of supreme interest. The young lovers' fate is not unmentioned because unimportant: but it was a question on which Thackeray clearly intended to be *led* as the situation evolved. (In the end, however, he was regrettably misled, submitting to a last-page union of Ethel and Clive in 'Fable-land' with a rueful: 'What could a fellow do? So many people wanted 'em married.')[9]

To finish this chapter I want to look at a scene which came off perfectly—the death of Colonel Newcome. With the help of the manuscript of the novel we can see this 'Euthenasia' as a prime example of the unforced and spontaneous complexity which is characteristic of Thackeray's finest writing. It may stand as representative of what is best in *The Newcomes*, as the death of Major Pendennis may stand for what is worst.

III

The last roll-call of Colonel Newcome is, with little Nell's death, the most famous scene in Victorian fiction. But unlike Nell's death Newcome's has rarely come to be thought of as merely curious or unintentionally funny by later readers. If the death-scene is not as tremendously effective as it was for contemporaries, nonetheless it is still admired. J .Y. T. Greig, normally the cruellest of critics, even goes so far as to praise it as an example of the Thackeray that might have been:

The famous death-scene is still famous, and deserves to be. If Thackeray had always written with such simplicity and restraint when a great occasion was presented to him, we, his readers of a century later, would have fewer doubts about his standing as a novelist.[10]

This is a long way from Oscar Wilde's inevitably repeated joke about one's needing a heart of stone not to laugh at the death of little Nell. One concurs; Greig's is earned praise (though one might cavil a little at 'simplicity and restraint'). Thackeray's handling of Thomas Newcome's euthenasia is, perhaps, the finest example of that emotional maturity which the great Victorian novelists could call on in their treatment of death: a maturity which, it has been observed, can go far to make up for what often seems like immaturity on sexual topics.[11]

There are two recorded anecdotes which testify that

Thackeray was intensely concerned, emotionally and artistically, with this climactic scene. The first relates to a street meeting between Thackeray and the American poet Lowell:

One day, while the great novel of *The Newcomes* was in course of publication, Lowell, who was then in London, met Thackeray on the street. The novelist was serious in manner, and his looks and voice told of weariness and affliction. He saw the kindly inquiry in the poet's eyes, and said, 'Come into Evans's, and I'll tell you all about it. *I have killed the Colonel.*' So they walked in and took a table in a remote corner, and then Thackeray, drawing the fresh sheets of manuscript from his breast pocket, read through that exquisitely touching chapter which records the death of Colonel Newcome. When he came to the final *Adsum*, the tears which had been swelling his lids for some time trickled down his face, and the last word was almost an inarticulate sob.[12]

The other anecdote is about the writing of the last scene. Thackeray had relied on the services of a secretary to whom he dictated much of *The Newcomes*. I have argued elsewhere that this mode of composition, especially where his daughter Anne was the secretary, had a deleterious effect on Thackeray's fiction.[13] But as regards Newcome's death Lady Ritchie recalls:

I remember writing the last chapters of 'The Newcomes' to my father's dictation. I wrote on as he dictated more and more slowly until he stopped short altogether, in the account of Colonel Newcome's last illness, when he said that he must now take the pen into his own hand, and he sent me away.[14]

What follows is the text of the great scene with Thackeray's corrections. The manuscript (which resides fittingly at Charterhouse) suggests strongly that Thackeray wrote only the one version of the scene—that as was his wont, he got it right first time. The scene is set in Greyfriars school (i.e. Charterhouse) where the ruined Colonel has retired as a humble pensioner:

he has just been visited by a young boy of the school and is obviously sinking fast.

After the child had gone, Thomas Newcome began to wander more and more. He talked louder: he gave the word of command and murmured 'Threes about and change' [changed, in proof presumably, to 'spoke Hindustanee as if to his men']. Then he spoke words in French rapidly, seizing |ETH| a hand that was near him, and crying 'Toujours, Toujours!' But it was Ethel's hand |AND HE DID NOT KNOW HER| ⟨which he took⟩. Ethel and Clive and the nurse were in the room with him; the latter [changed, in proof presumably, to 'nurse'] came to us, who were sitting in the adjoining apartment; Madame de Florac was there, with my wife and Bayham |AND MYSELF|.

|BY| ⟨At⟩ the look in the woman's |FACE| ⟨countenance⟩ Madame de Florac started up. 'He is very bad, he wanders a great deal,' the nurse whispered. |THE CHAPEL BELL BEGAN TO RING AT THAT TIME|. The French lady fell instantly on her knees, and remained rigid in prayer.

Some |MINUTES| ⟨time⟩ afterwards Ethel came in with a scared face to our pale group. 'He is calling for you again dear lady' ⟨she said⟩—going up to Madame de Florac who was still kneeling—'and just now he said he wanted Pendennis to take care of his boy. He will not know you.' She hid her tears as she spoke.

She went into the room where Clive was at the bed's foot—the old man within it talked on rapidly for a while—then again would sigh and be still—once more I heard him say hurriedly—'Take care of him when I'm in India;' and then with a heart rending voice he called out 'Eleonore Eleonore!'[15] She was kneeling by his side now. The ⟨patients⟩ voice sank into faint murmurs; only a moan now and then announced that he was not |SLEE| asleep.

At the usual ⟨evening⟩ hour the chapel bell began to toll, and |HIS| ⟨Thomas Newcome's⟩ hands outside the bed feebly beat a time |TO|. And just as the last bell struck—a peculiar sweet smile shone over his face, and he lifted up his head a little, and ⟨quickly⟩ said Ads [blotted] 'Adsum!' and fell back. It was the word we used

82

|TO USE| at school when names were called; and lo, he, whose heart was as that of a little child, had answered to his name, and stood in the presence of The Master.[16]

There are interesting minor improvements here: fine tuning adjustments which show that Thackeray wanted the scene to be polished as well as pathetic. But what is most interesting is that he originally intended to go from the nurse's whisper in the second paragraph to the chapel bell's tolling in the fifth (it is the sound of the bell, incidentally, which causes the devout Madame de Florac to throw herself to her knees). It was an afterthought, apparently, to cross out 'The chapel bell began to ring at that time' and postpone it so as to allow Léonore (the Colonel's first loved) to move from her pious station outside to Newcome's bedside. The afterthought develops into paragraphs three and four, which work up to the heart rending shout to the woman the Colonel still loves and the apparent collapse into final coma.

It was a daring stroke to unite these separated lovers and to remind us so forcefully, at this point, that they are lovers. Daring because it stresses that the Colonel dies with the married man's 'other—other thoughts' in his mind. It catches up a theme lightly touched on in an early, unusually frank, exchange between Clive and his father after the young married man has just seen Ethel:

'I have seen a ghost, Father' Clive answered. Thomas, however, looked alarmed and inquisitive, as though the boy was wandering in his mind.

'The ghost of my youth, Father, the ghost of my happiness, and the best days of my life,' groaned out the young man, 'I saw Ethel today. I went to see Sarah Mason, and she was there.'

'I had seen her, but I did not speak of her,' said the father. 'I thought it was best not to mention her to you, my poor boy. And are—are you fond of her still, Clive?'

'Still! once means always in these things, Father, doesn't it? Once means today, and yesterday, and for ever and ever.'

'Nay, my boy, you mustn't talk to me so, or even to yourself so. You have the dearest little wife at home, a dear little wife and child.'

'You had a son, and have been kind enough to him, God knows. *You* had a wife: but that doesn't prevent other—other thoughts. Do you know you never spoke twice in your life about my mother? You didn't care for her.'

'I—I did my duty by her: I denied her nothing. I scarcely ever had a word with her, and I did my best to make her happy,' interposed the Colonel.

'I know, but your heart was with the other. So is mine. It's fatal; it runs in the family, Father.' (879)

As he lies on his deathbed Newcome is mentally returned to India and the time when he was another woman's husband and Léonore another man's wife. It is not Mrs Newcome (the former Mrs Casey) that he calls to in his last moments. This rebellious 'spiritual adultery'[17] mixes oddly with the school-child's obedient 'Adsum.' The effect is complex: blank, childish innocence and adult passion combat in the Colonel to the very end. The novel finishes not only with a sanctified Victorian martyr going to receive his reward from the great schoolmaster in the sky but also with the image of a man doomed to an eternity of reluctant, sexual separation. The novel's epilogue was, in fact, to contain a similar image of separation: Clive (married to a more durable Rosey) denied Ethel. But here, unfortunately we may think, Thackeray gave in to his public's sweet tooth.

It is a flaw, for what one values most in *The Newcomes* are just such clear hard images of separation: Clive and Ethel aching for each other at the lecture on 'married bliss', the father miserable that his son loves him best when he is absent, the Colonel on his deathbed. To these Thackeray opposes conventional images of union: the gathered generations of a family praying in common Christian infancy to 'Our Father', Laura and Pen's bliss with their pious exclamations about 'the sanctity of marriage' and their baby a year, Colonel Newcome entering the kingdom of God as a little child.

Had Thackeray, as he seems to have intended, gone straight from the nurse's whisper to the final tolling bell, Newcome's passing from the world would have been no more than intensely saccharine and pathetic: the contradiction and with it the mixed effect would have been lost—or, rather, never found. As it is, a window is suddenly and dramatically opened onto the Colonel's secret life. There is no finer example of how Thackeray's sureness of hand and unplanned 'touches of genius' could transform the competent into the brilliant, the simple into the complex.

5

THE VIRGINIANS
The Worst Novel Anyone
Ever Wrote[1]

As Thackeray finished *Esmond* another novel sprang from it. Its germ is to be found in the afterthought 'Preface' where the Virginian Rachel talks of 'my two beloved boys. I know the fatal differences which separated them in politics never disunited their hearts; and as I can love them both, whether wearing the king's colours or the Republick's, I am sure that they love me, and one another' (xiii, 8). In these few maternal clucks is an embryonic sequel. Apart from Thackeray's temperamental love of fictional dynasty-making the direct inspiration of the sequel was twofold. As he came to the end of *Esmond* his mind turned naturally to America where Harry lives out his 'Indian summer' and which the novelist, as lecturer, was to visit in Autumn 1852. The other inspiration was not accidental, namely a continuing fascination with *Esmond's* 'revolution' theme and its 'crisis of loyalty' plot—how do men of good, but fixed, principles survive in these turbulent periods?[2]

To move from the 'preserving' English Revolution of 1688 to the 'preserving' American Revolution of 1776 was logical; to judge by a comment in his *History* Macaulay seems to have had the same inclination as Thackeray.[3] *The Virginians* continues the historical analysis of its predecessor while continuing the saga of the Castlewood–Esmond family. But the sequel is the vehicle for a historian's thinking much more than was

Esmond. It should be noted that Thackeray was increasingly thoughtful about history in the last ten years of his life;[4] and his lectures had given him a current reputation as a historian which he has since lost. No-one at the time seems to have thought it strange that he should have been nominated to finish Macaulay's *History of England*: and certainly the groundwork for *The Virginians* preserved in his notebook is more impressive in its scholarship than any other preparation he made for his fiction.

The scheme of *The Virginians* is familiar. The Warrington twins are versions of Thackeray's favourite idle and industrious apprentices, a source which is kept in our mind by occasional allusion.[5] Parts of the novel (particularly Harry's profligate career in England) can be seen almost entirely in the light of Hogarthian moral narrative. But there is another and original aspect to the dual-hero scheme. The basic 'idea' of the novel, forecast in *Esmond*'s preface, proclaimed on the novel's cover and declared in its first paragraph is that the Warrington twins fought on *different* sides in the American Revolution: 'The one sword was gallantly drawn in the service of the king, the other was the weapon of a brave and honoured republican soldier' (1). Disunited by cause, they were united in honour and, as their mother piously records, in love.

This honourable equivalence is, by design, a conciliatory approach—one which neutralises any ideological rancour. Both sides, Thackeray is saying, fought with honour and could shake hands after the conflict. The fact that men should have found themselves under one flag or another was, as with the congenital Warringtons, historical luck of the draw. Handy-dandy it could have been the other way round. As in school cricket all that matters is the spirit in which the 'game' was played: it is not honest partisans but 'sneaks' like Will who suffer the full weight of authorial odium.

As we shall see, there is little doubt that Thackeray wanted to mollify both his cis- and trans-Atlantic publics. Having an admirable hero in either camp ensured this. His letters 'To an American Family' suggest that the novelist may well have conceived a kind of diplomatic role for himself with *The Virginians* and it pleased him to joke on his prophetic middle name. The broker's role was made easier by his increasing scepticism about 'Revolution'. Unmistakable authorial sentiment lies behind George Warrington's confidence to his journal in chapter 90:

I pray my children may live to see or engage in no great revolutions, —such as that, for instance, raging in the country of our miserable French neighbours. Save a very, very few indeed, the actors in those great tragedies do not bear to be scanned too closely; the chiefs are often no better than ranting quacks; the heroes ignoble puppets: the heroines anything but pure. The prize is not always to the brave. In our revolution it certainly did fall, for once and for a wonder, to the most deserving: but who knows his enemies now? (962)

That Thackeray was a Laodicean on the subject of the 1688 settlement may be inferred from parts of *Esmond*, though in general he maintains a Macaulayan approval for the benefits flowing from the 'preserving Revolution'. In *The Virginians* his doubts are explicit: revolutions—the novel asserts—are perhaps necessary for progress and a good thing but life would be much more comfortable if they could be avoided.

One must regret, among other things, this explicitness in *The Virginians*. For what Thackeray has done is to geminate the taut, spiritual dilemma of a complex character like Esmond into the mere physical opposition of two simple characters. The Warringtons are not, properly speaking, twins but halves. A part of Henry Esmond yearned towards the old order of the Stuarts, another more rational part approved the Revolution and the Whig settlement: this with a similarly fissile love life makes Esmond's an infinitely rich characterisation. In *The Virginians* a parallel conflict is externalised in George the urbane loyalist versus Harry the robust republican. The externalisation might have been effective had the twins been allowed really to clash, but they are not. There is no heat in their opposition—one might almost say almost no opposition—only a gentlemanly and quite sparkless crossing of swords. We have Thackeray's testimony that this is a failure to execute what was planned. In conversation with J. E. Cooke in 1856 he said of his proposed Virginian novel:

I shall lay the scene in Virginia, during the Revolution. There will be two brothers, who will be prominent characters; one will take the English side in the war and one the American and they will both be in love with the same girl.[6]

The tension of lovers' rivalry was to be added to that of political difference so bringing things to an internecine, or as Rachel Warrington puts it 'fatal', pitch. Perhaps even a fight to the death or melodramatic sacrifice was envisaged. But in the written novel the romantic strand of the conflict was missed out, and the political strand strung so slack as to be boring. It is probably accidental that the part of the novel Thackeray failed to write in 1858 was written in 1859 by Dickens. The love rivalry of Carton and Darnay (twins in all but birth) is set centrally in a thunderous revolutionary context and brought to a perfectly timed climax.

The Virginians, though it hardly deserves Jerrold's apocryphal joke about its superlative badness, is Thackeray's worst major novel. Perhaps he waited too long to write it. The project was floating in his mind as early as the first American trip: 'tomorrow' he wrote to Lucy Baxter in February 1853 'I shall pass down the Potomac on which Mrs. Esmond Warrington used to sail with her two sons when they went to visit their friend Mr. Washington. I wonder will anything ever come out of that preface, and will that story ever be born?'[7] Then would have seemed the time to write it but in fact the work was not delivered until 1857, long after profitable gestation was over: it was apparently returned to as a second-best to J. J. Ridley's story, a sequel to *The Newcomes* which Thackeray wanted to write but for various reasons could not. As soon as he began *The Virginians* Thackeray regretted what he had embarked on, complaining that the work was: 'a horribly stupid story ... Don't tell me. I know better than any of you. No incident, no character, no go left in this dreary old expiring carcass.'[8] Such complaining is usual with him but in this case one is more inclined to agree than usual.

Having made these comments it is perhaps, vulturous to say that granted *The Virginians* is not Thackeray's best one is nonetheless grateful to have it as it is. Grateful because novels that go wrong often tell us most about an author's methods: the reader like the novelist learns from mistakes. Bearing in mind but often not mentioning the things that went right, the rest of this chapter will consider three problems which Thackeray failed to solve, which can be seen to contribute to the novel's breakdown but which, negatively, tell us much about his usual strengths. These may be termed, for shortness: (1) structural diffusion and confusion, (2) undue deference to American sensibilities and (3) moral insipidity.

II

From the modern reader's point of view the diffusiveness of *The Virginians* damns it. No Victorian novel is 'baggier' to use Henry James's term, or has less 'story' to use Thackeray's. Nowhere more appropriate is Thackeray's self-mocking description of his mulish Pegasus cropping the hedgerows when he wished it would soar. But we know Thackeray had a story in his mind when he began to write. Its outline is clearly there in the *Esmond* preface, the conversation with Cooke and the brief sketch notes he consigned to paper in his notebook:

Madam Esmond tries to dominate.
Her idea that people are in love with her.
Her respect for her elder.
Her passionate love for her younger son.
Her heroism during the siege.[9]

These minor episodes (not all were used) are small steps towards the major episode—Revolution and fraternal conflict. But Thackeray found it extraordinarily difficult to arrive at this central event. Extracts from his letters and other confidences record this difficulty as a chronic worry: 'I dawdled fatally between v. and x.';[10] 'the American part which was to have been in 12 numbers now has dwindled to 6—the construction of the story must perforce be altered'.[11] He might as well have said 'neglected', for it was not until after the *twentieth* number that he managed to arrive at 'the American part'.

It was not simply a case of dawdling, however. Thackeray's plans for the novel seem to have suffered from a confusion of aims. The simple action story designed to be set in Virginia at the time of the Revolution was crossed with another and quite uncongenial plot. Thackeray recalled it to a friend after a dinner party at John Forster's (Forster, incidentally, was a long-standing enemy of Thackeray's and had written a life of Goldsmith in 1848):

After the dinner at Forster's, Thackeray and Elwin left together. On their way home Thackeray talked of the Virginians, which was then in its early stages. He said he meant to bring in Goldsmith,—'representing him as he really was, a little, shabby, mean, shuffling

Irishman,'—Garrick—whose laugh he was positive he should be able to identify from the look in his portrait—Dr. Johnson and the other celebrities of the reign of Queen Anne.[12]

Garrick, Goldsmith and Johnson meant a setting of around the mid 1750s—that is to say some twenty years before the 'Revolution'. It also meant an emphasis on period description rather than the chronicling of any great historical event. To accommodate this second 'English' element Thackeray devised the subplot of Harry's visit to the Old World and his seduction there. He also worked out an elegant chronology: it was 1856 that he started work on *The Virginians: A Tale of the Last Century* so he began it exactly one century earlier and the novel begins (after the brief prelude which was inserted) 'One summer morning in the year 1756 ...' At the bottom of the second manuscript page Thackeray wrote '1736–1776' so indicating his intention to open with the first twenty years of the Warringtons' life which, as a flashback, makes up the first portion of the narrative.[13] The rest of the work was to concern itself with the next twenty years, 1756 to 1776, which would bring the action up to the period of the War of Independence. It was a beautifully symmetrical scheme but, as the man to whom he originally confided his plan records: 'Thackeray ... thought that he should find this easy, but he afterwards told Elwin that he had discovered he could not do it. The failure of his design threw him out, and the second half of the novel dragged for lack of materials.'[14]

Although Thackeray identifies the 'drag' as a feature of the second half of the novel, we can detect it much earlier than that. Take, for example, the opening. We recognise a familiar pattern—vividly dramatic first scene (Harry at Castlewood) followed by a long, looping flashback (the Esmonds in Virginia) which summarises all the necessary antecedent information for us, 'redoubling'[15] eventually to the starting point of the opening scene. It is Thackeray's usual gambit and a sound one. But if we convert the proportions of *The Virginians'* preamble into a ratio and compare this ratio with those of other novels some significant features emerge: *Vanity Fair* 1:1 (i.e. one chapter dedicated to the opening scene, and one to *resumé*), *Pendennis* 1:5, *Esmond* 1:5, *Newcomes* 1:3, *Virginians* 2:11.

It is hard to escape the impression that Thackeray is taking an exhaustingly long run up to the novel. This is not to say that the eleven chapters dealing with the Esmonds in Virginia are irrelevant: revolving as they do around three acts of juvenile 'rebellion' against 'domination' (as wielded by the tutor, the mother and the mentor) they admirably foreshadow the novel's intended crux. But it is Thackeray's narrative manner which is potentially disastrous; his own term 'dawdling' exactly describes it. Take these two passages on Madam Esmond's haughtiness: they occur within five pages of each other in the first number—the first number which, as Trollope pointed out to aspirant novelists,[16] should be the most incisive and brilliant in the novel since a score-or-so subsequent monthly sales depended on its gripping the reader:

Having lost his wife, his daughter took the management of the colonel and his affairs; and he gave them up to her charge with an entire acquiescence ... Of the Warrington family, into which she married, good Madam Rachel thought but little. She wrote herself Esmond Warrington, but was universally called Madam Esmond of Castlewood, when after her father's decease she came to rule over that domain. It is even to be feared that quarrels for precedence in the colonial society occasionally disturbed her temper; for though her father had had a marquis's patent from King James, which he had burned and disowned, she would frequently act as if that document existed and was in full force. She considered the English Esmonds of an inferior dignity to her own branch, and as for the colonial aristocracy, she made no scruple of asserting her superiority

93

over the whole body of them. Hence quarrels and angry words, and even a scuffle or two, as we gather from her notes, at the governor's assemblies at James Town. Wherefore recall the memory of these squabbles? Are not the persons who engaged in them beyond the reach of quarrels now, and has not the republic put an end to these social inequalities? (28–31)

The management of the house of Castlewood had been in the hands of the active little lady long before the colonel slept the sleep of the just. She now exercised a rigid supervision over the estate . . . The little queen domineered over her little dominion, and the princes her sons were only her first subjects. Ere long she discontinued her husband's name of Warrington and went by the name of Madam Esmond in the country. Her family pretensions were known there. She had no objection to talk of the marquis's title which King James had given to her father and grandfather. Her papa's enormous magnanimity might induce him to give up his titles and rank to the younger branch of the family, and to her half-brother, my Lord Castlewood and his children; but she and her sons were of the elder branch of the Esmonds, and she expected that they should be treated accordingly. Lord Fairfax was the only gentleman in the colony of Virginia to whom she would allow precedence over her. She insisted on the *pas* before all lieutenant-governors' and judges' ladies; before the wife of a governor of a colony she would, of course, yield as to the representative of the sovereign. Accounts are extant, in the family papers and letters, of one or two tremendous battles which madam fought with the wives of colonial dignitaries upon these questions of etiquette. (35–6)

The second passage is clearly redundant and in places verbally repetitious. All its information is conveyed in the first with the slightly irritating exception of the feuds between Madam Esmond and the local dignitaries whose details, it was earlier magnanimously decided, were not worth recalling. The passages follow so close on one another, within some 1,500 words, that every reader, even if he cannot exactly say

94

why, must find the second stale. We can see how it originally happened. Thackeray dictated the first description and penned the other himself: either he forgot during an interval in composition and repeated himself or was too busy fitting together fragmentary drafts to notice the overlap. But on re-reading he should surely have weeded out his narrative or have been less hurt when his publisher reported that initial sales were disappointing.

A favourite explanation of the shortcomings of *The Virginians* was that Thackeray had 'written himself out'. As an explanation it has the merits of simplicity and tallies with what we know of the novelist's generally dispirited condition at this time: but it is certainly wrong. Far from being written-out Thackeray had never, in the plain sense of the word, *written* better in all his life. The paradox is clearer if we consider some of the tributes which the work received, Gissing's, for example: 'Surely Thackeray's prose is much better in his later books than in the earlier. Two of the best passages he ever wrote are in *The Virginians*. The one is at the opening of chapter 29 on Idleness; the other, in chapter 31, in praise of wine.'[17] Yet Gissing does not suggest that *The Virginians* is a good novel because of the superior quality of its prose style. For writing at his best in this way often meant Thackeray's writing in such a way as to overload or neglect the narrative structure. With the aid of the manuscript we can actually see Thackeray elaborating scenes and passages so as to create this overloaded effect. One example will have to suffice; it is taken from the point in the narrative where Harry is disentangling himself from the dubiously virtuous dancer, Cattarina, and some other undesirable Tunbridge company:

In vain the mermaid's venerable mother waited upon Harry and vowed that a cruel bailiff had seized all her daughter's goods for debt. Harry left softer people than himself to pay the debt; and ordered Gumbo to mark the old lady well, and never admit her into his lodgings again. Having declined to play picquet any further with Captain Batts and being roughly asked his reason for refusing, Harry fairly told the captain that he only played with gentlemen who paid like himself.

This passage was enlarged at the proof stage thus:

In vain the mermaid's hysterical mother waited upon Harry, and vowed that a cruel bailiff had seized all her daughter's goods for debt, and that her venerable father was at present languishing in a London jail: Harry declared that between himself and the bailiff there could be no dealings; and that because he had had the good fortune to become known to Mademoiselle Cattarina, and to gratify her caprices by presenting her with various trinkets and knick-knacks for which she had a fancy, he was not bound to pay the past debts of her family, and must decline being bail for her papa in London, or settling her outstanding accounts at Tunbridge. The Cattarina's mother first called him a monster and an ingrate, and then asked him, with a veteran smirk, why he did not take pay for the services he had rendered the young person? At first, Mr. Warrington could not understand what the nature of the payment might be: but when that matter was explained by the old woman, the simple lad rose up in horror, to think that a woman should traffic in her child's dishonour, told her that he came from a country where the very savages would recoil from such a bargain; and, having bowed the old lady ceremoniously to the door, ordered Gumbo to mark her well, and never admit her to his lodgings again. No doubt she retired breathing vengeance against the Iroquois: no Turk or Persian, she declared, would treat a lady so: and she and her daughter retreated to London as soon as their anxious landlord would let them. Then Harry had his perils of gaming as well as his perils of gallantry. A man who plays at bowls, as the phrase is, must expect to meet with rubbers. After dinner at the ordinary, having declined to play piquet any further with Captain Batts, and being roughly asked his reason for refusing, Harry fairly told the captain that he only played with gentlemen who paid, like himself. (300)

In the rewriting there has been a distinct improvement: vitality and sharp detail have been added, bare description has become vivid scene. There are some twenty such passages evident from the manuscript. In themselves they do not add more than ten pages to the length of the printed book, but if we regard them as indicative of the author's general tendency can we be surprised that the novel has a certain lack of forward thrust? For in these passages, as above, Thackeray stops to embroider and in so doing drops the main narrative thread. Harry's purity with regard to Cattarina and the gamblers has already been made clear in the earlier action, there is no need to reiterate it here other than that Thackeray was beguiled by the opportunity of a lively digressive scene.

These passages, I repeat, do not in themselves make much difference to *The Virginians* but regarded as symptoms they tell us much about what has gone wrong with the novel.

III

Incidental finesse abounds in *The Virginians*: it is a treasure house of what the Victorians liked to hoard as literary 'gems'. None of Thackeray's novels has finer passages of commentary, more delicate touches of comedy or pathos, mellower or wiser egotising, defter historical colouring or purer 'Saxon', as *Harper's Magazine* called it.[18] *The Virginians* contains Thackeray's finest illustrations and some of his best verbal vignettes: one at least (Baroness Bernstein unrecognisable beneath Beatrix's portrait) is as famous as anything the novelist wrote. Gordon Ray's loan word from impressionist painting, *pointillisme*,[19] is exactly right to describe the prose texture of *The Virginians*. As appropriate is the epithet 'classic' which was increasingly applied to Thackeray's style in his later years; the Latin chapter titles (which the novelist uses all the way through) aptly confirm this quality in the novel. Nowhere more than in *The Virginians* is Thackeray the *arbiter elegantiarum* that Trollope recommended to every tyro stylist.[20]

A price is paid. The novel is unjointed and disproportioned. It does not go where it should. In fact it often goes nowhere at all: the American editor of *Harper's* was forced to apologise three times to his readers for *The Virginians'* lack of plot (the desire for *story* was surely 'childish' he concluded with more hope than certainty).[21] Thackeray's letters show that the novelist was conscious of this as a fault. His manuscript shows that he made occasional efforts to control the drift; jumps in page numbers bear witness to amputation, episodes are arbitrarily cut short (this is especially noticeable in George's prison narrative, which was very much altered and hacked about), and finally there is the abrupt shift to autobiographical narration in the last quarter of the novel. By removing an editorial filter Thackeray presumably hoped to get a faster narrative flow. But these sporadic attempts to wrench the novel into shape are hardly impressive and one wonders if Thackeray really cared, beyond a little tinkering, about the structure of *The Virginians*. Necessity and probability are blithely sacrificed to episode and the narrative is jerked along by unworthy tricks of plot— impossible coincidences, unexpected inheritances, convenient arrests and releases, dead men resurrected, even the hoary old solve-all of the last page discovery of lost legal documents.

Saintsbury in his edition offers the interesting suggestion that *The Virginians* shows Thackeray discovering his identity as an essayist, an identity he was to cultivate in his later career, and that as in *Tristram Shandy* progression is fatally distracted by digression. (Thackeray actually included a Shandean joke in *The Virginians*, George's *History of the Revolution* which he can never get round to writing.) Saintsbury's is a persuasive but ultimately unverifiable suggestion and we are left with a paradoxical novel. The nature of the paradox was neatly summed up by Meredith, perhaps himself taking warning for his imminent entry into the ranks of the great novelists. After the third number of *The Virginians* Meredith enthused in a letter: 'Ah! how charmingly *The Virginians* is written. W.M.T. is the most perfect artist in Prose that I know of.'[22] When the work was finished he concluded, all enthusiasm spent: 'where there is no plot, no story, the author generally maunders. Look at *The Virginians* where [Thackeray] is forced to depend entirely upon character, and overworks it, distends it, makes it monstrous.'[23]

IV

Some aspects of *The Virginians* which are deferential to trans-Atlantic sensibilities have already been noted. Others stand out prominently. The reader cannot but notice that the novel opens with a florid compliment to a distinguished American friend. Neither will he miss the fact that the best Englishman in the novel, Sir George Warrington, is an expatriate American or that all the villains come from the 'wicked selfish old world' or that for the first two hundred pages there is not an Englishman who does not swear, wench, booze, gamble immoderately or cheat at play.

Thackeray knew a good deal about Americans' prejudices and their touchiness where the national image was concerned. Dickens's earlier mauling must have been in his mind and he had felt a pretty sharp tap himself for a trifling remark about General Washington in the opening chapters of *The Newcomes*.[24] Two lecturing trips to America had brought Thackeray into personal contact with Americans, whom he liked more than Dickens had, and it was doubtless a matter of affection as well as professional efficiency to know them and

99

to understand what allowances should be made in addressing them. That he did make allowances can be shown with an almost clinical precision. The lectures on the *Four Georges* which provided the material for the '56 lecture tour (and much of *The Virginians'* English background) exist in two versions: there is the manuscript text from which Thackeray addressed his American audience and the text printed for British readers in 1861. The differences are striking and systematic. The lectures which the Americans heard contain prominent diatribes against old-world royalty, aristocracy and the rank system generally. Many of these references are toned down or removed altogether for English readers.

From the evidence of these deletions we may gather that Thackeray developed what amounted to an evasive strategy for his American lectures. The 'wicked nobleman' is presented as a shared arch-enemy whom the middle class Englishman (that is Thackeray) may detest as legitimately as his republican audience. The aristocratic or royal bogeyman-cum-Aunt-Sally is then satirically clubbed and both sides are happy.

What this evasive strategy meant in practical terms for Thackeray was, in effect, a return to the satirical methods of his hot-blooded, lord-baiting youth. This is evident if we consider three brief passages thought suitable for American ears but not, presumably, for English eyes: the first is an aside from the lecture on George I:

Here in America your unfortunate education has deprived you of the benefit of understanding that great difference which existed, and even still exists in many parts of the European continent between the *Adel* or *noblesse*, and the common people. In a well regulated principality in Germany you may still see the army officered by noblemen—at the theatre the noble society sits apart from the citizen society; to be a merchant, a lawyer, a doctor, is still almost an eccentricity among persons of noble blood.[25]

The next example is also from the lecture on the first George and also concerns European morals and politics:

. . . the tradition is not yet extinct in Europe. Gouty old Poloniuses still stand behind royal chairs; delicate maids of honor [*sic*] may not always sit whilst healthy young Princes are taking their tea. The game keeper loads the gun and hands it to the gentleman in waiting who hands it to H.R.H. who then fires at the pheasant or the grouse. If any of you were present as myriads were at that splendid pageant, the opening of our Crystal Palace in London, you might have seen one noble lord act as hat-holder—as peg for H.R.H.'s cocked hat while his speech was being read.[26]

The third passage is from the lecture on George III, the monarch who, in the printed text, is the Hanoverian paragon. It refers to the sending of convicts to north America after the Revolution:

After that fine note of the poor King's comes another equally characteristic respecting the sending over of convicts to Nova Scotia. 'Undoubtedly' says the King, 'the Americans cannot accept and will not receive any favour from me: but the permitting them to receive men unworthy to remain in this Island, I certainly consent to.' Does not one see the rage of the man, the stolid spite, and abiding hatred? His armies are beaten. Those hated rebels are triumphant. The wolf would not be shorn. One can imagine how the thought lashed his blood into fury and disturbed his wavering reason.[27]

One can as well imagine how soothing such passages were to American ears. Nor can it have been hard for Thackeray to produce them: all that was required was a lapse into old ways. Snobonomy rides again: the second of the above extracts is a revamping of the satire on the Prince Consort's hunting practice in the fourth chapter of the *Snobs of England* and the whole conception of the *Four Georges* stems, as Saintsbury points out, from a lampoon written in 1845.[28] The animus behind the lectures, shown at its plainest in the suppressed passages, can be seen as a revival of the republican enthusiasm which had led the young Thackeray into some excessive satire on the nobility.

One should make the point, however, that Thackeray was not being merely irresponsible and mercenary in the *Four Georges*. Like many thinking Englishmen he was appalled by the administrative incompetence shown up by the Crimean War and, again like many thinking Englishmen, blamed it on the political aristocracy. In the mid-fifties he was active in the Administrative Reform Association with Dickens, and as did Dickens, used the satirical force of his pen to back up his political convictions.[29] The *Four Georges* can be seen to originate in the same indignation which created the aristocratic Barnacle family with their network of civil-service sinecures in *Little Dorrit*. But there were differences: Dickens did not take his protest abroad for gain and combine it, as did Thackeray, with praise for American public figures so incurring the charge that, as one enemy put it:

No one succeeds better than Mr. Thackeray in cutting his coat according to his cloth: here he flattered the aristocracy, but when he crossed the Atlantic, George Washington became the idol of his worship; the 'Four Georges' the objects of his bitterest attacks.[30]

Another and more important difference was that Dickens was strong and consistent in his views. After the initial flush of anger Thackeray's opinions moderated and he came to think badly of his Hanoverian lectures. The verdict of his artistic conscience is recorded in a letter of December 1856 to the wife of the publisher John Blackwood where he confessed that he finds lecturing 'not wholesome or dignified or pleasant— only lucrative'.[31]

1. 'Mr. Osborne's welcome to Amelia.' (*See pp.* 11–17.)

an utter silence in his gorgeously well-furnished drawing room only interrupted by the eternal ticking of the great French Clock. When that Chronometer (filled for us in a heavy Cathedral tone) with its tremendous voice struck 6 it said a cheerful train group of faithfully sacrificing —

Mr Osborne pulled the bell at his right hand violently, and the butler rushed up.

— Dinner, roared Mr Osborne.

— Mr George is not come in sir, interposed the man

— Damn Mr George sir — am I master of the house? DINNER! Mr Osborne scowled. Amelia trembled — a telegraphic communication of eyes passed between the other three ladies — the obedient bell in the lower regions began ringing the announcement of the meal.

The tolling over, the head of the family thrust his hands into the great tail pockets of his great blue coat, and without waiting for a further announcement strode down stairs alone, scowling over his shoulder at the four females.

'What?' the mutter now ran (in an undertone) one of the others as they tripped behind the Sire.

I suppose the French are beginning whispered Miss Wirt; and so trembling and in silence this hushed female company followed their dread leader. They took their places in silence. Two rows of candles were lighted, the great silver dish covers were removed — Amelia trembled in her place, for she was alone next to the awful Osborne, and alone on her side of the table, the gap being occasioned by the absence

2. A page from the *Vanity Fair* manuscript (*See pp.* 11–17.)

3. A Thackeray sketch for *Vanity Fair* (i) (*See pp.* 18–22.)

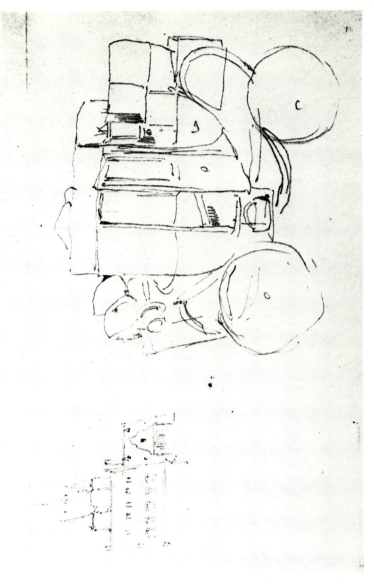

4. A Thackeray sketch for *Vanity Fair* (ii) (*See pp.* 18–22.)

5. The Waterloo number notes (*See pp.* 18–22.)

6. 'Rebecca makes acquaintance with a live Baronet.' (*See p.* 43.)

7. 'How "Boy" said "Our Father".' (*See p.* 85.)

THE VIRGINIANS

A TALE OF THE LAST CENTURY.

BY W. M. THACKERAY.

Author of " Esmond,"
" Vanity Fair,"
" The Newcomes,"
&c. &c.

LONDON:
BRADBURY AND EVANS, 11, BOUVERIE STREET.
1857

8. The monthly cover of *The Virginians* (*See p.* 87.)

9. The monthly cover of *Pendennis* (*See pp.* 113–14.)

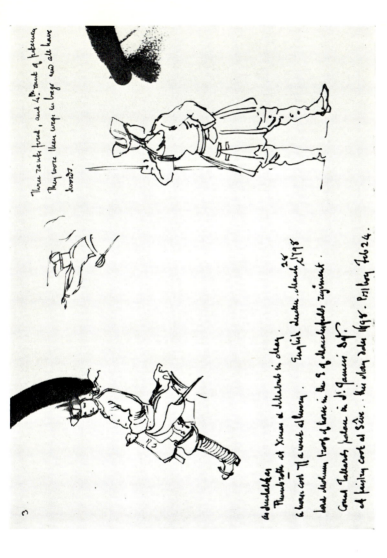

10. A page from the *Esmond* notebook (*See p.* 117.)

eyes and read :—" Dearest ! Mamma's cold is better this morning. The
Joneses came to tea, and Julia sang. I did not enjoy it, as my dear
was at his *horrid dinner*, where I hope he amused himself. Send me a
word by Buttles, who brings this, if only to say you are your Louisa's
own, own," &c. &c. &c. That used to be the kind of thing. In such coy
lines artless Innocence used to whisper its little vows. So she used to
smile ; so she used to warble ; so she used to prattle. . . . ~~Under~~
my windows, as I write, there passes an itinerant flower-merchant. He
has his roses and geraniums on a cart drawn by a quadruped—a little
long-eared quadruped, which lifts up its voice, and sings after its manner.
When I was young, donkeys used to bray precisely in the same way ;
and others will heehaw so, when we are silent and our ears hear
no more.

Insert A

A

A Young people, at present engaged in the pretty sport, be assured your middle-aged parents
have played the game, and remember the rules of it. Yes, under Papa's bow-window of a
waistcoat is a heart ~~that~~ which took very violent exercise when that waist was slim. Now
he sits tranquilly in his tent, and watches the lads going in for their innings. Why, look
at Grandmamma in her spectacles reading that Sermon. In her old heart there is a corner
as romantic still, as when she used to read The Wild Irish Girl or the Scottish Chiefs in the
days of her misshood. And as for your Grandfather, my dears, you to see him now you would
little suppose that that calm polished dear old gentleman was once as wild—as wild as
Orson. . . Under my window, &c !

11. Thackeray 'sermoning' in *Philip* (*See p.* 117.)

V

Indignation about aristocratic administrative incompetence and deference to American susceptibilities may both be felt combining to affect *The Virginians*. This is not surprising: it was written immediately after the American trip and early impressions were sold to *Harper's* for almost simultaneous publication. And, of course, the novel took as its proposed main action a highly controversial episode in American history at the same time that Thackeray was exercised about a controversy on how English society ought to be run—by the middle classes and merit or the upper classes and privilege? We can hardly fail to note, for example, that the novel begins and ends with the chronicles of military campaigns bungled by armies 'officered by noblemen'. Here the influence of the Crimean débâcle and the public debate it provoked can be seen directly to inspire some of the novel's most vigorous writing and thinking. And at a second remove the same inspiration could be found behind the satirical portraiture of the Castlewood family who first insult, then trap in marriage and finally rob their less scheming American cousins.

The dualistic design of *The Virginians*, which had been conceived as early as 1852, demanded an even-handed treatment from Thackeray. He should have scrutinised the New World as unblinkingly and harshly as the old. But the balance was tipped: first by the novelist's current anti-aristocratic sentiments in the mid-fifties, secondly, and more insidiously, by a disinclination to offend his American readership. On this second score there are some tell-tale erasures evident in the manuscript of the novel. Descriptions of Franklin and Washington which might offend are cut or toned down. Accounts of the conduct of certain parties in the Revolution are changed so as to cause no annoyance. Some praise of Benedict Arnold,

the arch-traitor, is removed. In a number of places references to
negro slavery are rendered neutral—the hint for example, that
white ladies spited their husbands by taking black lovers is
struck out. As with the previous illustrations of narrative
expansiveness these are not in themselves substantial but straws
indicative of the wind's direction.

In one sense Thackeray's deference was merely, and under-
standably, tactful. Americans were rightly fed up with clever
British authors who accepted their hospitality and went home
to publish lucrative satires on the New World. American
accounts of England, *Harper's* complained, in the same editorial that welcomed Thackeray's contribution, had been
'thoughtful, instructive, just, admiring and generous'; English
accounts of America 'captious, undiscriminating and unjust'.[32]
But in other ways, ways which cannot be excused as literary
good manners, one suspects Thackeray may have comprom-
ised his integrity as a historian and his instinct as a satirist.
Consider as what is, I think, a substantial piece of evidence the
description of General Braddock's campaign which follows.
Had Thackeray allowed it to stand it would have come early in
the story, during the build up to George Warrington's 'death'
in the ill-fated military expedition to Fort Duquesne:

This veracious narrative contains the history not of Virginia or
North America, but of a couple of Virginian gentlemen and so I am
luckily spared from uttering the words of blame which a historian
and moralist must have uttered in this place on this subject. A
hundred years ago there existed among the two millions of in-
habitants of the British North American provinces some folks
whose breed | OF COURSE HAS | ⟨has fortunately⟩ died out and who
were [Here the passage breaks off: Thackeray starts to rewrite it on
the same page.]
The efforts made by the provinces were not particularly | BRILLIANT |
⟨energetic⟩. In fact they seemed inclined to let the British Govern-

ment fight their battle, | CONTRIBUTED | fulfilled none of their en-
gagements, and contributed neither men nor money nor horses
nor beef. |so THAT|The British general broke up his congress of
Governors in a fury. Maryland and Virginia on which he had
counted for his conveyance and a great portion of his provision,
brought him only twenty waggons and two hundred wretched
horses ⟨Pennsylvania was absolutely unprepared to give horses or
men⟩ until Mr. Benjamin Franklin informed his fellow citizens that
the General would take what he wanted by force, if he could not get
it by fair payment on which the Pennsylvanian farmers found
horses and waggons.[33]

The hesitancy is given away by the stopping and starting,
the generally apologetic manner and the manifest difficulty in
finding the right adjective. But having written it with difficulty
Thackeray found it prudent to remove this passage altogether
and replace it with a version which completely altered the
historical judgement. In the revised version the 'blame' for the
reluctant loyalty of the colonists is shifted from their inherent
stinginess to the excesses of the brutal British soldiery who
'swaggered the country round, and frightened the peaceful
farm and village folk with their riot'. It is this license (especially
to respectable women), not the natives' inclination 'to let the
British Government fight their battle' which accounts for the
non-cooperation in the matter of war supplies.

It is reasonable to assume that the deleted account contains
Thackeray's honest historical opinion of the conduct of the
thirteen states, especially of Pennsylvania, in the campaign of
1755. There are only a handful of such revisions in the manuscript of *The Virginians* and one should not, I repeat, build
too much on them alone. But it seems likely that the whole
work was composed in a spirit of precaution: that Thackeray
rarely let himself get to the stage of being indiscreet, even in
his manuscript.

But despite his care Thackeray found it impossible to avoid scraping American sensitivities. This was particularly the case with Washington who figures prominently in the early part of the novel as a somewhat cold, but otherwise impeccable, friend of the Warrington family. The very inclusion of the father of the nation in a novel was, however, too much for some readers. One such wrote indignantly to *Harper's* denouncing *The Virginians* as literally sacrilegious:

Do you know that legions, who have been the ardent admirers of *Harper*, feel, just now, 'largely aggrieved' because Thackeray is writing about Americans, holding up in a ridiculous light the *most honorable name* our country can boast? No American writer has ever had the *impiety* to attempt a novel with the revered George Washington figuring in it as 'some vain carpet knight'.

Every true American will feel shocked. Next to making the Saviour of the world figure in a modern novel, would be placing in such light the 'Father of his Country'. Next to ridiculing religious feeling, is striking at the veneration for the *great and good* with the subtly poisoned pen of ridicule.[34]

Harper's replied by suggesting that their angry correspondent should wait to see how the whole portrait would turn out. It was not a particularly good reply for immediately after this fuss Thackeray left American affairs and the American setting out of his novel for 600 pages. As a result his novel designed to be set 'in Virginia during the Revolution' has little more than a tenth of its bulk devoted to that time and place. We have seen that the subsequent Goldsmith–Johnson–Garrick plan was a distracting factor; but it seems more than likely that the premature removal of the action from America (in chapter 14) and the dilatoriness in getting it back there (in chapter 85) and on to the Revolution was as much due to a disinclination to stir up controversy with his American readers.

VI

This leads naturally to the third consideration, moral insipidity. It seems that Thackeray wanted to write a novel about marriage and its problems rather than *The Virginians*: he had originally intended, he told his friend Elwin, 'to show J.J. [Ridley—the painter in *The Newcomes*] married, and exhibit him with the trials of a wife and children. I meant to make him in love with another man's wife, and recover him through his attachment for the little ones.'[35] Having begun this work Thackeray found he could not go on with it, so he burned the manuscript and turned to his 'tale of the last century', a project which had been on the stocks for several years. His first instinct was sound. The kind of novel he proposed with J.J.'s story is that which was just on the horizon with George Eliot and which was to dominate English fiction until the end of the century. From *Middlemarch* and *The Ordeal of Richard Feverel* to *Portrait of a Lady* and *Jude the Obscure* the analysis of unhappy or incompatible marriage is an area of main interest to the novelist. Instead we have *The Virginians* which, under its stylistic glaze, reaches only the shallowest of psychological levels.

Thackeray must have felt this shallowness as a deficiency. How else can we explain a small and otherwise irrelevant appendix in chapter 85, a confidence from George to his journal? The manuscript shows that it was written after and inserted into the previously finished chapter.[36] George is musing on his life's rewards:

What admission is this I am making? Here was the storm over, the rocks avoided, the ship in port and the sailor not over-contented? Was Susan I had been sighing for during the voyage not the beauty I expected to find her? In the first place, Susan and all the family can look in her William's log-book, and so, madam, I am not going to put my secrets down there. No, Susan, I never had secrets from thee.

I never cared for another woman. I have seen more beautiful, but none that suited me as well as your ladyship. I have met Mrs. Carter and Miss Mulso, and Mrs. Thrale and Madam Kaufmann, and the angelical Gunnings, and her Grace of Devonshire, and a host of beauties who were not angelic, by any means; and I was not dazzled by them. Nay, young folks, I may have led your mother a weary life, and been a very Bluebeard over her, but then I had no other heads in the closet. Only, the first pleasure of taking possession of our kingdom over, I own I began to be quickly tired of the crown . . . I yawned in Eden, and said, 'It this all? What, no lions to bite? no rain to fall? no thorns to prick you in the rose-bush when you sit down?—only Eve, for ever sweet and tender, and figs for breakfast, dinner, supper, from week's end to week's end!' Shall I make my confession? Hearken! Well, then, if I must make a clean breast of it.

*   *   *

Here three pages are torn out of Sir George Warrington's MS. book, for which the Editor is sincerely sorry. (904–5)

As a taste of what might have been it is tantalising. George seems about to confess that even in a happy marriage love atrophies making the best of husbands Bluebeards, at least in their private worlds. It is, as George Eliot would have said a tragedy which has no significance other than its frequency. The odd passage juts out as a small reminder of the unhappy-marriage novel Thackeray began but could not carry through and which he replaced with *The Virginians*. Momentarily the novel touches that 'real business of life' which Thackeray, wrongly I think, claims can 'form but little portion of the novelist's budget.'[37]

VII

There are a number of reasons for being dissatisfied with *The Virginians*. It has too much fine writing and not enough organisation. It misjudged the mood of the age and was weakened by an authorial demoralisation well reflected in a letter: 'This note if I go on I feel will be very glum. The Virginians is no doubt not a success. It sadly lacks story, and people wont care about old times, or all the trouble I take in describing them.'[38] And in trying to please too many and offend nobody *The Virginians* is generally insipid, the more so with *Adam Bede* and a new moral toughness emerging in fiction. Here, more than anywhere, one accepts the full severity of Trollope's judgement:

For desultory reading, for that picking up of a volume now and again, which requires permission to forget the plot of a novel, this novel is admirably adapted. There is not a page of it vacant or dull. But he who takes it up to read as a whole, will find that it is the work of a desultory writer, to whom it is not unfrequently difficult to remember the incidents of his own narrative. 'How good it is, even as it is!—but if he would have done his best for us, what might he not have done!' This, I think, is what we feel when we read the *Virginians*. (138)

6

DENIS DUVAL
The Serialist and the Scholar

Denis Duval appeared as Thackeray's third serial for *The Cornhill*, the monthly magazine whose figurehead he was. He had about a half of his novel written and part of it set up in type when he died. Correcting these proofs was the novelist's last literary act: he died, as did Dickens, chained to the serialist's oar. But the astonishing feature of *Duval* is that there is nothing tired about it, it promises in fact a recovery in age of the powers of youth.

Duval tells the story of a young refugee from France born in 1763 and raised in an *emigré* Protestant community at Winchelsea. The portion of the novel which reached final composition is narrated by Denis in later life, 'long after the voyage is over, whereof it recounts the adventures and perils'.[1] Fortunately Thackeray managed to complete what is a set-piece in all his novels, the account of the hero's childhood, spent in this case among south-coast smugglers and fishing folk. As a parenthesis to Denis's upbringing we are given the tragic family history of Agnes de Saverne, his childhood sweetheart and later his wife. Agnes's father, we learn, was killed in a duel and her mother, whose honour was at stake, has run mad. The course of the subsequent plot is laid by introducing a set of villains (who, like Mohun in *Esmond*, are historical)—principally the duellist-lover La Motte and the lower bred Weston brothers. The fact that (historically) La Motte was hanged for espionage and the other two were highway robbers suggests the direction the story would have taken. The novel as it is printed breaks off with Denis joining the navy. This was to have introduced an eventful nautical career for the adult hero before he finally reached the conventional haven of happy marriage.[2]

Slight as the eight chapters that we have are, we can learn a lot by observing how Thackeray set to work on *Duval*. First, as the corrected page proofs show, he intended to start publishing with only a few chapters in hand.[3] This gap would probably have narrowed to the point where, after a few months, Thackeray was only days or even hours ahead of his monthly deadline. Such forwardness was his normal practice, and Dickens's too—with the difference that in later life Dickens evidently had a better idea of where he was going. Thackeray was more of Trollope's party: 'when I sit down to write a novel I do not at all know, and I do not very much care, how it is to end.'[4] Recognising this waywardness in himself Trollope cautiously kept his work until it was complete: when he died his unfinished novel was found in a drawer. Thackeray left in his desk drawer the promissory note: 'I. O. S.[mith] E.[lder] and Co. 35 pp.'[5]

Thackeray, the London Horace, is nowhere less Horatian than in this question of holding back his work.[6] Consequently he backed his powers of invention even more than Dickens. Serialisation meant for Thackeray a monthly gamble on his creative stamina and it is common to see in his letters the pious suffix '(DV)' after references to the 'next number'. The strain was the greater for him in mid-career when he had, as he lamented, 'taken one crop too many out of his brain'[7] and, we may suspect, his body. During an ongoing serial a famous novelist's reputation was at risk every month. He was not only sensible of the opinions of critics who could revise first judgements at leisure and of readers who could register their displeasure by withdrawing their subscription (sending him letters to explain why) but even his friends would be watching every number, waiting for the tell-tale signs of exhaustion. A comment of John Blackwood's to G. H. Lewes indicates the monthly tribunal which the serialist was forced to undergo:

He says he cannot get ahead with *The Virginians*, and was desperately pushed with the last [Number], having written the last sixteen pages in one day, the last he had to spare. The last two [Numbers] are, I think, better than their predecessors, but he must improve much or the book will not keep up his reputation.[8]

Especially when he felt this kind of thing was going on behind his back Thackeray's temper could flare and he would break out in unaccountable rages against quite innocent parties.

The serialist's was not, as Motley pointed out in one of his letters, an enviable condition:

I can conceive nothing more harassing in the literary way than [Thackeray's] way of living from hand to mouth. I mean in regard to the way in which he furnishes food for the printer's devil. Here he is just finishing the number that must appear in a few days. Of course, whether ill or well, stupid or fertile, he must produce the same amount of fun, pathos or sentiment. His gun must be regularly loaded and discharged at command. I should think it would wear his life out.[9]

It is an appropriately desperate image that Motley finishes with. But the image Thackeray himself offered to Macready is, perhaps, more to the point:

I am behindhand with my work in consequence of repeated fits of illness with which of late I have been knocked over and want to try and make a rally next month and get a couple of numbers ahead . . . otherwise it is more than probable that the at-present flourishing firm of The Virginians will have some day to stop payment.[10]

But Thackeray rarely managed to get ahead of himself and invariably suffered at what he called 'the struggling time of the month'.[11]

Clearly the precipitate method adopted for all but one of his novels invited the criticism that he was playing the *improvisatore* without Dickens's prodigious energy to sustain the part nor, apparently, the other novelist's 'elbow-grease of the mind' (Trollope: 122) to direct it. Indeed Trollope lays the blame for the slackness of Thackeray's fiction squarely on his surrender to the 'seductive' temptations of serialisation. And to some degree Trollope is right. When writing *Pendennis*, for example, Thackeray found the story coming on so well that at about the thirtieth chapter he decided to expand the novel's size from twenty to twenty-four numbers. This arbitrariness can be related to what most readers feel as faults in the novel: Pen's childhood and youth at Fairoaks is allowed to fill seventeen chapters then, with a palpable jerk in the narrative, Thackeray realises that he is lingering, so Pen's university career at Oxbridge is hurried over in a third of the space with the apology, 'We are not about to go through Pen's academical career very minutely' (211). Thereafter for every step forward the plot moves two steps sideways into a digressive sub-plot. In the preface to the novel (in fact an afterword) Thackeray tells us of a certain 'plan' which was 'put aside' (xxxvi). That such was indeed the case is evident from the way that around the twenty-fifth chapter there are clear anticipations of Helen's death and Blanche Amory's disreputable parentage.[12] Thackeray does not normally forecast distant plot developments and we may suspect that the main action was to hinge on the Madonna's death and the Siren's surprising ancestry. In fact the one is reserved for the emotional climax of the novel (chapter 57) the other for its denouement.

Another false lead is evident in the cover to the monthly

issue of *Pendennis*. Thackeray did not normally give much clue as to plots of his novels in these illustrations (which were, of course, available to the reader from the first number onwards) but that for *Pendennis* is unusually explicit. Here, manifestly, Thackeray has committed himself to future plot elements and far from helping him these hostages to the monthly reader were extremely embarrassing. In the written novel he did not manage to arrive at the love-conflict suggested on the cover until well into the novel's second half (a delay which has led one ingenious critic to propose Major Pendennis as the mermaid).[13] Some of the reason for the delay in setting up the Blanche-Laura tug-of-war over Pen can be deduced from a letter Thackeray sent Mrs Brookfield in August 1850:

... At the train whom do you think I found. Miss [Gore] who says she is Blanche Amory, and I think she is Blanche Amory, amiable (at times) amusing, clever and depraved. We talked and persifflated all the way to London; and the idea of her will help me to a good chapter, in which I will make Pendennis and Blanche play at being in love, such a wicked false humbugging love, as two blase London people might act, and half deceive themselves that they were in earnest. That will complete the cycle of Mr. Pen's worldly experiences, and then we will make, or try and make, a good man of him.[14]

A train journey, a chance encounter, a happy inspiration and everything falls into place. But what if Thackeray had not met Miss Gore? Would we have more of the dullness which everyone, including Thackeray, finds in the novel's latter stages? Does this not bear out Trollope's rule that 'A novelist cannot always at the spur of the moment make his plot and create his characters who shall, with an arranged sequence of events, live with a certain degree of eventful decorum, through that portion of their lives which is to be portrayed' (52)? And can we disagree with the objection which the *Fraser's* reviewer made against *Pendennis*?

We have remarked another defect in the texture of the story, namely, a want of uniformity. About the middle, the thread is spun out to the last degree of tenuity; towards the end, we have a complication and entanglement of incidents. The author at one time lingers and languishes, at another rushes on with feverish haste to reach the goal in time. Perhaps his own illness may have been the cause. Yet he should have remembered a precept of his favourite Horace, *Primo ne medium, medio ne discrepet imum.*[15]

II

Serialisation aggravated the tendency of Thackeray's fiction towards shapelessness. So much may be conceded Trollope. But he is wrong to assume, as he does, that there was never anything in the way of germinal or preparatory activity. In *Duval*, for example, there was a layout stage which Thackeray called suggestively, 'sketching'. In the notes for the novel we have, at the very beginning, this longest note 'Sketch for a Story' (it is, incidentally, virtually the only note in the pocketbook which concerns the 'story' as such):

I was born in 1764 at Winchelsea, where my father and everybody else was a good deal occupied with smuggling.

There used to come to our house a noble French gentleman called the *Count de la Motte*, and with him a German the Baron de *Lütterloh*. My father used to take packages to Ostend and Calais for these gentlemen and perhaps I once went to Paris and saw the French Queen.

The Squire of our town of Winchelsea was Squire *Weston* of the Priory, who with his brother kept a genteel house and was Churchwarden of the parish.

Now if you read the Annual Register of 1781 you will find that on the 13 July the Sheriffs of London attended at the Tower to receive custody of *M. de la Motte* charged with treasonable correspondence with the enemy.

Under pretence of sending prints to France and Germany, he had been accustomed to supply the French Ministry with accounts of the movements of the English ships and troops. His go-between was Lütterloh a Brunswicker who had been a crimping agent for supplying Hessians for the American war, then a servant, then a spy of France and Mr. Franklin and who turned king's evidence on la Motte finally and hanged him.

And in 1782 came on at the Old Bailey the trial of [the Westons] for the robbery of the Bristol mail in 1780 when nothing appearing to prove their guilt, they were acquitted, but tried immediately after on another indictment for forgery. Joseph was acquitted, and John capitally convicted: but this did not help Joseph. Before the trial these two with others confined in Newgate broke prison, and Joseph fired a pistol on a porter who tried to stop him in Cheapside. For this he was found guilty by the Black Act and hung along with his brother.[16]

There are two immediately interesting features in this plot projection. The first is the far-reaching nature of Thackeray's 'sketch': he is thinking a long way ahead—further, in fact, than he managed to bring the action in the few months of life that remained to him.[17] The other interesting feature is the tentative and delicate manner in which Thackeray explores the distant possibilities of his unwritten story—'sketching' is a term which aptly describes it. To talk of Thackeray, as he talks of himself, sketching for his novels is, of course metaphorical. But it is a metaphor which aptly catches the deft, probationary way he worked into his fiction and the triggering processes which got the plot into motion. Pen and pencil sketching, so called, throws up fluid situations valuable for the stimulation they gave Thackeray's imagination. Their effect on the novelist is not one of containing by framework but of liberating by suggestion. And the term 'sketch' registers the outset of the solidifying and enlarging process by which the novel came alive under Thackeray's hand. (*Duval's* sketch was originally for a story of a 'hundred pages'.)[18] The interpenetration of pen and pencil sketching as far as Thackeray himself was concerned may be gathered from the reproduced page (pl. 10) of the *Esmond* notebook where prosaic and pictorial detail are jumbled all together.[19]

III

To return to the genesis of *Duval*. At an even earlier stage than that of the germinal sketch the novel began with a cold-bloodedly professional decision to write something different from the domestic, hum-drum realism of *Philip*. But *Duval* was not the first 'different' story thought of: in what now seems like a perverse affront to his talents, Thackeray originally intended to write a historical novel set in the period of Henry V whose action was to involve the grandsires of his most famous heroes.[20] Two or three pages of notes for this saga are found preceding those for *Duval*. That he should have entertained such a bizarre enterprise (hardly less bizarre than the rumour circulating London at the time that he was writing an Anglo Saxon novel)[21] confirms his intention to write something with more 'story' and less indulgence of the famous 'sermoning'. The eventually preferred *Duval* setting with its smuggling, war and continental intrigues was almost certainly chosen to serve the same intention. But in the event the desired stress on 'story' was not achieved by simply adopting the formula associated, since Scott and Dumas, with historical romance: 'an incident in every other page, a villain, a battle, a mystery in every chapter'.[22] Thackeray's other eighteenth-century fictions, *Esmond* and *The Virginians*, offered adventure plots set in periods of historical turbulence and yet turned out to be among the most sententiously long-winded of the author's novels. *Duval*'s concentration on 'story' was achieved, rather, by the creation of a *dirigiste* narrator into whom, as a conscious assumption of role, Thackeray projected himself. One notes, for example, that the sketch begins not 'Denis Duval is' but, dramatically, 'I was'. It is a significant detail. Thackeray had learned very early in his career that to narrate a work of fiction entailed acting the part of a narrator, especially when (as in all his novels to some extent) the action is set in the historical past. There is a revealing anecdote on the subject told by the American actor Lester Wallack who performed before Thackeray in an eighteenth-century period drama and

when the piece was over Mr. Blake and I went into the green-room and were introduced to Thackeray by my father, who knew him intimately in London. I remember his saying: 'I have seen tonight an illustration of what I have preached over and over again, the endeavour of the artists to remember that they are presenting, not only in personal appearance but in *manner*, the picture of what is past and gone, of another era, of another age almost, certainly of another generation.'[23]

It was this sense of *acting* his narration, narrating by *manner*, as he says, which I suspect led Thackeray to dictate much of his work. Hodder, the most efficient of his amanuenses, offers another illuminating recollection which pictures Thackeray holding the actor's disciplined facial mask as he dictates:

He never became energetic, but spoke with that calm deliberation which distinguished his public readings; and there was one peculiarity which, among others, I especially remarked, viz., that when he made a humorous point, which inevitably caused me to laugh, his own countenance was unmoved, like that of the comedian Liston, who, as is well known, looked as if he wondered what had occurred to excite the risibility of his audience.[24]

The histrionic elements in Thackeray's narration owe an obvious debt to his beloved eighteenth-century humorists, particularly Fielding. But they owe as much to the literary circumstances of his own century. Thackeray's professional career was begun in the anonymous pages of periodical journalism. He quickly discovered that the only way to establish an identity within this anonymity, identity which would allow him to build a reputation and bargaining power with his paymasters, was distinctive pseudonymy. The opening sentence of the *Yellowplush Correspondence* (Thackeray's first sizeable fiction) conveys the exuberance with which he threw himself into the part of the pseudonymous narrator:

I was born in the year one, of the present or Christian hera, and am, in consquints, seven-and-thirty years old. My mamma called me Charles James Harrington Fitzroy Yellowplush, in compliment to several noble families, and to a sellybrated coachmin whom she knew, who wore a yellow livry, and drove the Lord Mayor of London ... (i, 168)

Yellowplush was a great popular success but there was no need in the later fiction for anything as brash as this. Nonetheless a certain histrionic poise remained vital to Thackeray's narration. He was himself quite conscious of it: writing in a letter he observed of *The Newcomes*:

Mr. Pendennis is the author of the book, and he has taken a great weight off my mind, for under that mask and acting, as it were, I can afford to say and think many things that I couldn't venture on in my own person, now that it is a person, and I know the public are staring at it.[25]

Gaseous but low-pressured Pendennis was right enough for the leisurely and talkative novels he presents. But Thackeray, as we have seen, wanted something more lively for *Duval*: hence 'I was'. We can show, however, that this brisk 'I was' was worked for and arrived at only after experiment and various wrong turnings. The surviving papers for *Duval* reveal that

Thackeray began by writing a novel narrated by a biographer-editor—a thinly disguised Pendennis, in fact. Fragments of this false opening, up to the seventh page, have been preserved or can be excavated from under various crossings-out.[26] A few extracted quotations will serve to demonstrate the tone and manner of this *Ur-Duval*:

... Mr. Duval was never without a pleasant word and a merry laugh. And there he'd sing so blithe and jolly, like another Tom Bowling. In the tranquil little town you could hear his merry voice, singing French songs and English and even high Dutch, as he worked in his garden. It was said he could speak or sing in all three languages equally well. At church every Sunday it was fine to hear him join in the morning hymn: and no church in all Christendom could show a more stately pair than the old warrior and his wife who faithfully frequented its services and now lie side by side under its wall, | NOT DIVIDED IN DEATH AFTER A LIFE OF STEADFAST AFFECTION, WHO RISE UP FROM THE GRASS AND LIVE AGAIN AS THEIR BIOGRAPHER'S OWN BOYHOOD REVIVES AMID SCENES FEELINGS FRIENDS FONDLY REMEMBERED | ... Do you wonder that I should know these details? My dear Madam in that dear old town of Fareport, they used to talk about Admiral Byng's trial, about Captain Cook's voyages, about the ghost which came to Lord Lyttleton at Hagley, about the Gordon riots, about the Black Hole at Calcutta, as commonly as people now do about spirit rapping or the battles in America—the elders talked that is; the young sate and listened and remembered. In manhood we may forget but who does not remember childhood and its pangs and its pleasures?

Thackeray sensed that this opening with its time- and death-conscious 'biographer', writing in the present (see the comment on the 'battles in America') was wrong: too slow and melancholy. But this realisation did not come until he had gone a long way down the narrative *cul-de-sac*. He improved on the draft we have quoted and produced a fair-copy chapter written in the person of the biographer which perfected the reminiscential vision and easy pace of its predecessor. Although Thackeray suppressed this prelude it survives and has been printed.[27] Its gentle tone may be sampled from the first and last sentences of the opening paragraph:

Over the back of the arm-chair in which I sit, I remember as a boy how there used to hang a little, slim, powdered queue which dear old Dr. C. wore . . . Good readers, if you will listen to a story of old times, I will relate one which must have come to pass when this old chair was new.[28]

The suppressed first chapter of *Duval* is one of the finest of Thackeray's many dissertations on time, 'the silver-wigged charioteer'[29] (a pencil-drawing of the old man can be seen on the back of the first MS. sheet.) Nonetheless, despite the autumnal beauty of the chapter, it would not do. It was too slow and flatulent, too much in the way of the story. So Thackeray cut the biographer and rewrote instead a convulsively abrupt and autobiographical opening. This began with a barrage of facts:

The persecution of Protestants by Lewis XIV drove many families out of France into England, who have become trusty and loyal subjects of the British Crown. Among these thousand fugitives were my grandfather and his wife. They settled at Winchelsea in Sussex, where there has been a French church ever since Queen Bess's time and the dreadful day of St. Bartholomew . . .[30]

It was on the right lines but too sudden. So finally Thackeray settled on a compromise: he allowed himself five sentences of reminiscential introduction (borrowed in slightly modified form from the first 'biographical' draft) before breaking into his story as above with what I have called the 'abrupt' opening. And this compromise version is the one which finally saw print:

To plague my wife, who does not understand pleasantries in the matter of pedigree, I once drew a fine family tree of my ancestors, with Claude Duval, captain and highwayman, *sus. per coll.* in the reign of Charles II, dangling from a top branch. But this is only my joke with her High Mightiness my wife, and his Serene Highness my son. None of us Duvals have been *suspercollated* to my knowledge. As a boy, I have tasted a rope's-end often enough, but not round my neck; and the persecutions endured by my ancestors in France for our Protestant religion, which we early received and steadily maintained, did not bring death upon us, as upon many of our faith, but only fines and poverty, and exile from our native country. The world knows how the bigotry of Louis XIV ... (3)

IV

Some interesting features emerge from this evolution. Primarily one notes that the exacting process of trial and error was undertaken not in any spirit of grim laboriousness but rather one of mounting excitement. Thackeray's mood is caught in the draft of a letter he scrawled out to his publisher, George Smith:

My Dear Smith,

I have had my great Cheval de Bataille in training for the last fortnight and was just going to mount him for Agincourt, but I have a *wild* story in my mind which I might work into 100 pages of the magazine ...[31]

The other notable feature is the artistic self-discipline which is shown in the progressive devising and discarding of drafts. Thackeray was ready to sacrifice some very fine writing in order to reach effects which he felt to be exactly right—more particularly a narrative voice and manner which was exactly right. (It is interesting, by the way, that Thackeray found he could not dictate Duval's lively narrative as he had the 'confidential talk' of Pendennis).[32] Doubtless some of the sacrifices were painful. The following fine digression about the seducer La Motte's fatalistic philosophy was, apparently, suppressed:

Is it fate which impels the man, or is it man who brings the fate down on him? We spake anon of the fruit of the tree which our first mother ate, and which caused the downfall of all our race. Yes, but the tree was there and the fruit hung tempting within reach. No tree, no temptation, it might have been; had Wisdom not ordained otherwise. I knock my head against that trunk often and often. Good Mr. Harrison our vicar of Fareport has not made the matter clear to me. As for the Chevalier de la Motte, he always professed to think he had no more control in the matter than Punch has in the Show. He is a puppet pulled by hands under the Curtain . . . Then my man may knock my brains out, and steal my spoons with a tranquil mind, saying that to these things among the rest he was ordained. And then, if he is also ordained to be hanged . . . Well, well. The matter is for gentlemen of the Church. But I vow in this walk through life we seem to meet with men foreordained to evil bringing on themselves and those near them wrath and grief and ruin. Such a man was this Chevalier de la Motte of whom two and well nigh three persons in one family (I know not how many more) were the victims.[33]

One appreciates this as vintage Thackeray. Doubtless he liked it also, but it was too expansive so it was shrunk down to a single exclamation by la Motte on the irresistibility of 'Fate'[34] and the reader denied one of Thackeray's sermons on free will.

Thackeray was not always as strict with his hobby-horses as here in *Duval*. But when he is at his best narrative problems are worked out in a spirit which, though mercurial, is anything but slapdash. Some of the notes for Thackeray's prematurely concluded novel were published in *The Cornhill* to refute, as the editor said: 'a too-hasty notion which we believe to have been pretty generally accepted: namely, that Mr. Thackeray took little pains in the construction of his works'.[35] Trollope, characteristically, hacked into this 'evidence' with a ruthlessness worthy of Chaffanbrass himself:

[Thackeray] could go down to Winchelsea, when writing about the little town, to see in which way the streets lay, and to provide himself with what we call local colouring. He could jot down the suggestions as they came to his mind, of his future story. There was an irregularity in such work which was to his taste. His very notes would be delightful to read, partaking of the nature of pearls when prepared only for his own use. But he could not bring himself to sit at his desk and do an allotted task day after day . . . he was a man of fits and starts, who, not having been in his early years drilled to method, never achieved it in his career. (57)

On the evidence published in *The Cornhill* Trollope is right enough in his strictures. But had he realised the pains that went into tuning a voice for the first chapter of *Duval* Trollope would surely have amended those hard words about Thackeray's 'idleness' in preparing for the novel. And if 'fits and starts' means the ability to stop and begin again rather than doggedly ploughing a barren furrow one cannot but be glad that Thackeray suffered the handicap.

V

While he was working out how to tell his story Thackeray was also busily acquiring collateral material for *Duval*. This was undertaken in a number of ways. First, as Trollope contemptuously notes, he steeped himself in the locale of the novel, sniffing round odd corners of Winchelsea and Rye, sketching the town architecture, hunting out characteristically regional names. Hence we find this entry in the early pages of the notebook:

|RYE| ⟨Winchelsea⟩ had 3 gates. New gate on SW, Land Gate NE. and Strand Gate SE leading to Rye.
W. Church of St Thomas of Canterbury.

The Govt was vested in a Mayor and 12 jurats. Jointly it sends canopy bearers on occasion of a coronation.
Pecock's School at Rye.
Holloway's Rye or Sussex?[36]

This insinuation into the physical situation of his novel, inhabiting its world, was a necessary procreative act for Thackeray.[37] As *Esmond* was forming in his mind he told his mother, for example, 'I have been living in the last century for weeks past.'[38] Some of the notes for *Duval* show him once again living in the eighteenth century:

I helped to clean the boat, to get the lines in order, I was taught to steer in fine weather (with many a rap on the head when I got her in the wind) and having very keen eyes at that time for marks distances bluffs headlands and the like knowing them instantaneously when first they loomed through the mist and remembering them afterwards I was used as lookout boy and to give notice of ships or revenue cruisers in sight . . . We would pull out a certain distance, and taking cross bearings sink our kegs and leave them quietly till a more convenient time, and then we would drag for them and bring them up with line and grapnel.[39]

It is possible that the above is a memorandum for a fragment of narrative (though in the story Denis does not often serve with the smugglers). But what seems more likely is that the passage is an exercise in which Thackeray deliberately soaks himself in Denis's world, savouring its objects and language. This 'second sight'[40] seems to have been an invariable prelude to composition.

One should not, however, suggest that Thackeray was permanently in a trance-like state of negative capability. Years of hurried deadlines and pressing publishers had made him opportunist enough to exploit the specialised knowledge of others. Though he could go to Rye and imagine himself as the youthful Denis in a fishing boat he could not, as he lamented, 'take a journey in a man-of-war so as to learn all the nautical phrases'.[41] He therefore milked the information from those who had (among them an Admiral). The following letter is typical of others:

My dear Fonblanque. I am a little boy born in the year 1763 at Winchelsea where my parents lived, having been expelled from France after the Revocation Edict of Nantes, which I suspect brought the Fonblanques to England too.

My Grandfather was Precentor and Elder of the French Church at Winchelsea, a perruquier by trade, but a good deal engaged in smuggling. I went upon various smuggling expeditions; but as I don't know the difference between a marling spike and a binnacle, I must get information from somebody as does, and who knows better than you?

Three or four sentences will be enough to tell me and write them like a bold seaman as you are for

Yours ever
W. M. Thackeray.[42]

Since Thackeray laced the proofs of *Duval* with some dense nautical material we may assume that his charming request was acceded to by Fonblanque. Sometimes, too, the novelist would leave 'blanks' for this kind of technical information and when he had the services of an amanuensis would often send him off to fill them in.[43]

Letters like the above are particular instances of a general alertness. Thackeray seems always, in one corner of his mind at least, to have been on the *qui vive*. Several commentators record his carrying his manuscripts on his person. Dr Brown tells us why: 'he was continually catching new ideas from passing things, and seems frequently to have carried his work in his pocket, and when a thought, or a turn, or a word struck him, it was at once recorded'.[44] Dickens, writing Thackeray's obituary in *The Cornhill*, testifies that *Duval* had been subjected to this same peripatetic improvement: 'the condition of the [MS. pages shows] that he had carried them about, and often taken them out of his pocket here and there, for patient revision and interlineation'.[45] And as well as studying the world about him the serialist had a unique opportunity of studying his own public. The close contact which monthly composition fostered between author and reader could, at its best, create fascinating cross-fertilisations. In his review of the first numbers of *Vanity Fair*, for example, Abraham Hayward petitioned that Rawdon Crawley should not die, as seemed inevitable, but should be allowed to live in exile as a British Consul somewhere in Africa or South America.[46] Thackeray, who was grateful for an enthusiastic review obliged and made Rawdon the Governor of Coventry Island—and then had him die there. But the most famous example of Thackeray's responsiveness to his readers' suggestions was the dinner conversation which, unexpectedly, furnished the brilliant 'puppetry' ending of *Vanity Fair*:

It occurred in June, 1848, one day when Thackeray came at lunchtime to my father's house. Torrens McCullagh, happening to be one of the party, said across the table to Thackeray, 'Well, I see you are going to shut up your puppets in their box!' His immediate reply was, 'Yes, and, with your permission, I'll work up that simile.'[47]

This kind of lucky find could happen only with a writer whose novel was never quite out of his mind: the image Thackeray applied to himself in this interesting condition is the obvious one:

... for the last ten days I have been almost *non compos mentis*. When I am in labour with a book I don't quite know what happens. I sit for hours before my paper, not doing my book, but incapable of doing anything else, and thinking upon that subject always, waking with it, walking about with it, and going to bed with it. Oh, the struggles and bothers—Oh, the throbs and pains about this trumpery![48]

But as well as having pains Thackeray took them. The acquisitions which prior research furnished for his fiction and his countless hours in the British Museum Reading Room are not usually appreciated—certainly not by Trollope. It is perhaps as well they are unappreciated: our enjoyment of *Esmond* would not be enhanced by an awareness of Smollett's *History of England*, Abel Boyer's *History of Queen Anne*, the *New Atalantis*, Macpherson's *Original Papers*, Howell's *State Trials*, etc. Novels do not carry bibliographies gracefully. But the fact that we cannot smell the oil does not mean, as Trollope assumes, that none was burned. On one page of the *Duval* notebook Thackeray cites as sources: the *Gentleman's Magazine* 1769 and 1782 (three references), Vol. x of the *Sussex Archaeological Collections* (on smuggling), *Sessions Papers* 1782 (on the Westons), *Notes and Queries* Series 1, Vol. x. To go to the British Museum and call up these sources (they will be the same volumes that Thackeray used) is to earn the right to a hollow laugh at one aspect of Trollope's charge of idleness.

Especially in the historical novels which make up more than half of his major work Thackeray was assiduous in his research. But brainwork is moulded so discreetly into the fictional matter that it rarely protrudes to remind the reader of itself. His skill in this and, more importantly, his restraint may be shown by juxtaposing half a page of notes with a paragraph from *Duval* which they enrich:

Refugees. At Rye is a small settlement of French refugees who are for the most part fishermen and have a minister of their own, 1685.

After the massacre of St. Bartholomew a large body of F.P.'s took refuge here as did others on the revocation of the E. of N. Murray 248.

Wherever there is a suffict. number of faithful there is a church.

The pastor is admitted to his office by the provincial synod or the colloquy provided it be composed of 7 pastors at least.

Pastors are seconded in their duties by laymen who take the title of ancients (Elders) and Deacons. Precentor.

The Union of Pastors, Elders and Deacons forms a Consistory.

Ein fester Burg ist Unser Gott

Ein gute Wehr und Waffen.[49]

The world knows how the bigotry of Louis XIV drove many families out of France into England, who have become trusty and loyal subjects of the British Crown. Among the thousand fugitives were my grandfather and his wife. They settled at Winchelsea, in Sussex, where there has been a French Church ever since Queen Bess's time and the dreadful day of St. Bartholomew. Three miles off, at Rye, is another colony and church of our people: another *Fester Burg*, where, under Britannia's sheltering buckler, we have been free to exercise our father's worship, and sing the songs of Zion. My grandfather was elder and precentor of the Church of Winchelsea, the pastor being Monsieur Denis, father of Rear-Admiral Sir Peter Denis, Baronet, my kind and best patron. (3-4)

Each of the notes is introduced into the paragraph below but in a tactful and unostentatious way. A less tactful writer would surely have pulled in all the jargon about precentors, hierarchical titles and so-on, or have labelled Luther's hymn so no-one could miss his erudition or his wit.

Trollope's misrepresentation of this kind of notebook material as 'local colouring' or 'pearls' is mischievous. It is not a case of Thackeray tricking out his fiction. Rather it is the putting of a scholarly intellect to the service of his imagination in capturing the texture of Denis's background. The notes may be, as Trollope says, irregular—but nonetheless there is a logic in them. We may draw the same conclusions from the *Esmond* notebook where the entries are not worked as directly into the novel but are nonetheless *there*:

Statue of the Kg. in *Stocks Market*. The neatly wrought Conduit in the Market Place: at the West End of Lombard St., whereupon is placed a very magnificent statue of K.C.II on Horseback trampling upon an enemy all in white marble at the sole cost of that worthy Citizen and | BARONET | ⟨Alderman⟩ Sir R Viner Knt and Bt.

In King's Square—Soe. Hoe Fields Buildings is another statue of the King very fine.

Fleet Brook. The mighty chargeable and beautiful work rendering navigable the Fleet Brook a Ditch from the river Thames up to Holborn Bridge; the curious stone bridge over it, the many huge vaults on each side thereof to treasure up Newcastle coals for the use of the poor.

Exchanges. There be many exchanges in London besides Markets and the Royal Exchange—as that stately building called the New Exchange and Exeter Change both in the Strand ⟨where all attire for ladies and gentlemen is sold⟩—not to speak of the Cloysters of Saint Bartholomew and others.[50]

The end result of these painstaking notes is not to be found in such incidents as that in book three where the hero goes to the 'Change to buy Beatrix a ribbon. What these notes show is Thackeray methodically reconstructing Esmond's world which he must imaginatively inhabit if he is to write Esmond's story. Hence the emphasis on topography and the affectation of writing as his hero's contemporary ('There *be* many exchanges . . .').

The notion of Thackeray acting his narration, presenting by *manner* as he told Wallack, is again relevant. This historical reconstruction is exactly the preliminary exercise Stanislavski recommends in 'Creating a Role'. The actor must mentally concretise not just his 'part' but his part's environment, his house, his society. But one does not have to go as far as Stanislavski for the key to Thackeray's method, more particularly the enthusiastic miscellaneity of his method. It is to be found in the connection with his friend, the historian Macaulay.

Macaulay's practice of totally immersing himself in a period in order to write its history was famous. An extract from his journal illustrates it well:

I have now made up my mind to change my plan about my History. I will first set myself to know the whole subject; to get, by reading and travelling, a full acquaintance with William's reign. I reckon that it will take me eighteen months to do this. I must visit Holland, Belgium, Scotland, Ireland, France. The Dutch archives and French archives must be ransacked. I will see whether anything is to be got from other diplomatic collections. I must see Londonderry, the Boyne, Aghrim, Limerick, Kinsale, Namur again, Landen, Stein-kirk. I must turn over hundreds, thousands of pamphlets. Lambeth, the Bodleian and the other Oxford libraries, the Devonshire papers, the British Museum, must be explored, and notes made: and then I shall go to work.[51]

It was, as Trollope might have objected, 'irregular', but irregularity with a method. 'The chief advantage of these re-searches,' Macaulay noted, unconsciously echoing Thackeray's words while conceiving *Esmond*, 'is that the mind is transported back a century and a half.'[52] And while writing *Esmond* Thackeray ruefully compared himself with Macaulay: 'it takes as much trouble as Macaulays History almost and he has the vast advantage of remembering everything he has read, whilst everything but impressions—I mean facts dates and so forth—slip out of my head, in which there's some great faculty lacking, depend upon it.'[53] What he meant by this 'great faculty' is ex-pressed in his obituary tribute to Macaulay, surely the most graceful ever penned. It is worth quoting at some length be-cause it describes, albeit ideally, the synthesis of diverse material which Thackeray attempted in his own field, historical fiction:

Well—take at hazard any three pages of the 'Essays' or 'History':— and, glimmering below the stream of the narrative, as it were, you, an average reader, see one, two, three, a half-score of allusions to other historic facts, characters, literature, poetry, with which you are acquainted. Why is this epithet used? Whence is that simile drawn? How does he manage, in two or three words, to paint an individual, or to indicate a landscape? Your neighbour, who has *his* reading, and his little stock of literature stowed away in his mind, shall detect more points, allusions, happy touches, indicating not only the prodigious memory and vast learning of this master, but the wonderful industry, the honest, humble, previous toil of this great scholar. He reads twenty books to write a sentence; he travels a hundred miles to make a line of description. (xvii, 363)

Thackeray was recognised, by his contemporaries at least, as Macaulay's natural successor after the great *History* had been cut short by death. That he would have continued in the same spirit as Macaulay, 'absorbing' rather than cramming facts he himself vouched.[54] And the British Museum Reading Room— 'that catholic dome in Bloomsbury, under which our million volumes are housed' (xvii, 364)—where they both spent so much of their working lives, Thackeray saw as the necessary storehouse for Macaulay's *magnum opus*. It is not entirely hyperbolic to say the same of *Esmond, Vanity Fair, The Virginians* and *Denis Duval*. The period manner of these novels, their historical 'feel' are a distillation of the greatest library in the world.

Appendix One:
The Local Plans for *Denis Duval*

I have been unable to locate a complete set of plans for any Thackeray novel and I doubt whether any were ever made. But especially towards the end of his life it is evident that Thackeray would make occasional plans, of a kind, for the future plot and character developments of his novels and that these were thrown away as soon as they had served their immediate purpose. They were not, for example, kept like the other historical notes in a bound pocket-book but jotted down on any handy piece of blank paper. Some of these plans have been luckily preserved, more often than not thanks to some zealous relic hunter. For the second chapter of *Duval* there survives a projection, incomplete and on what is obviously scrap-paper but as far as it goes plotting the immediate narrative course in close detail. It should, perhaps, be mentioned that the chapter is extremely complicated in its exposition of the family background of the Savernes:

A description of Nancy and Stanislas's court.
One of his Chamberlains was M. le Marquis de Saverne, an amiable extravagant man who had already injured the family property.
He had three daughters and a son, the gloomy Count de Barr.
The Marquis de Saverne had a house at Nancy; and a house at Saverne, near which the Archbishop of Strasbourg also had a palace.
The Hotel de Saverne at Saverne was given up to the Count de Barr on his marriage with a kinswoman of his own.

They had awful disagreements.

More than once Madame de Barr fled from Saverne to her father in law at Nancy. She was terrified to have to go back to her husband. He was of a furious and ungovernable temper but withal deeply religious and full of remorse for the violence which he showed in his fits of jealousy and anger.

For a while there were no children and he thought the barrenness of his wife a punishment from heaven for his passionate behaviour. At length after some time of marriage Mme. de Barr became in an interesting condition. The idea of having a child *softened* the grim father immensely. What should he do to provide for his son? He saved pinched went in shabby clothes would do anything for the child. The old father sneered at his impetuosity, his wife wearied alike of his attentions and his fits of anger. From which you may suppose that she was thinking of someone else besides M. de Barr.[1]

(This plan was expanded in the writing, the hint in the last sentence developed, M. de Barr absented at war during his wife's confinement and the flight to England added.)

On the back of an old letter (dated 29 November 1863— some thirty days before Thackeray's death) is another plan for the novel, sketchy but with a wider sweep:

I recover. I am informed that I am [to be] entered as a first class volunteer. The captain has written home to say what has befallen me. My mother comes off to the ship with money, uniforms, and a chest for me. She brings me a letter from Dr. Barnard. I wait upon the Captain who continues his kindness to me. We get orders to sail Serapis. We put into Ostend. My imprisonment and recognition by some of our smuggling associates. Return to England.[2]

This is, properly speaking, less a plan than a syllabus. It shows Thackeray listing the main events for the next hundred-or-so pages of his story which death was to forestall his writing. Other such skeletal outlines and *aides memoires* have been preserved but not enough to make absolutely certain whether the exercise were a normal or unusual practice. Yet it is likely that the foregoing plans are representative of many others which have perished.

Thackeray, as has been said, kept a notebook for *Duval* as well as making these apparently isolated plans. In the notebook he entered details from his reading for the novel and its eighteenth-century background. Thackeray's research was wide-ranging and many of the entries tend to be miscellaneous or random-seeming. The impression one has is of a mind concentrated on the task of preparation yet constantly alive for incidental distraction. Consider the following extract from page 16 of the notebook where Thackeray can be seen consulting newspapers of 1777 for the military history and yet is as interested in the advertisements as the news ('M.P.' is *The Morning Post*, 'Chron' is *The London Chronicle* and 'Gaz.' is *The Gazetteer*; all three volumes are bound in the 1777 volume of the Burney collection of periodicals in the British Museum):

The Exeter Diligence was stopped and robbed by a highwayman. Gaz. Ju. 10. 77.
The king had the best private information regarding the movements in the French ports. M.P. June 13. 77.
D.H. was a man with mean talents and a bad heart. As a writer he was contemptible indifferent to truth and honesty, a shallow scribbler who has dishonored the name of letters, and who will in due time be gathered to the dull of ancient days. Gazetteer June 13. 77.[3] An American privateer showed her stars and stripes in Southampton Water 4 June 77 Chronicle 14 June
tickets to Carlisle House balls 1½ guineas. Chron 16 June 77.
John Wall DuVal Dancing master in X St. Hatton Garden, taught the minuet and country dances and cotillons.

Other parts of the notebook can be found which relate more directly than this to *Duval*, as we know it from the printed text.

On pages 11, 14 and 15 the following entries occur:

Jo. W. always savage against Blaise—[i.e. Denis] fires on him in Cheapside. (11)
Martha the maid gives the information to M. de Saverne at Boulogne, and frightened at the catastrophe which ensues returns to her own friends in France. (14)
The ball entered a little to the right of the middle of the breast bone, penetrated the lung and the large artery supplying it with blood, and caused death by immediate suffocation. (15)
1779. 9 July. Kings proclamation announces that the French intended to invade these kingdoms. One Sunday at Church on the sea coast the panic was so great that every body ran out of church except the clergyman and two or three people. Campbell 5. 471. (15)[4]

These notes correspond with events in the novel. In chapter 5 Joseph Weston, disguised as a highwayman holds up the coach Denis is riding in to London (though in fact Denis fires on *him*). In chapter 3 Martha, at Boulogne, betrays her mistress's whereabouts to the Count. The medical description of the Count's cause of death is to be found, *verbatim*, in the surgeon's report at the end of chapter 3. The description of invasion panic taken from Campbell, is adapted with Dr Barnard playing the part of the intrepid clergyman in chapter 8 (see page 127). All four of these correspondences are to be discovered in the notebook surrounded by other less relevant or entirely irrelevant detail. This suggests that the ideas were jotted down as they came to the novelist spontaneously while he was working on *Duval*'s background.

Most interesting of the relevant entries is the following from page 10:

Old Blaise   b. circa   1740
Blaise b.   1763
Henriette de Barr was born in 1766–7
Her father went to Corsica   68

Mother fled	68
Father killed at Be.	69
Mother died	70
Blaise turned out	79
Henriette *Iphigenia*	81
La Motte's Catastrophe	81
Rodney's action	82

Blaise and Henriette are early versions of Denis and Agnes. Thackeray does not use these discarded names in the manuscript so one can assume that the chronological plan, given here, precedes the final draft of the early chapters. One may also assume that Thackeray had some major spans of his plot already thrown in his mind. Agnes was to be sacrificed like Iphigenia (presumably in marriage to Lütterloh), the story was to work to a simultaneous climax with naval action ('Rodney's action') and nemesis for the villain ('La Motte's catastrophe'). Taken together with the 'Sketch for a story' (pages 5–6 of the notebook) this chronological plan demonstrates that there was a pre-existing framework for the narrative.

In chapter 8, the last that Thackeray wrote, Denis is about to go to war in the Serapis, commanded by Captain Pearson. Historically this vessel was taken by Paul Jones off Scarborough in one of naval history's most famous battles. In the last page of the notebook Thackeray wrote 'Qy. how did Pearson get away from Paul Jones?' Thackeray's query obviously concerns Denis's escape as well. Appropriately enough Thackeray seems to have ended his career still wrestling with the problem of the unwritten instalment.

Appendix Two:
The *Esmond* Notebook

Thackeray was by temperament a scholarly author and read widely in the eighteenth century for his historical novels and lectures. It was his habit to keep notes from his reading, usually of a more or less random nature, in leather-bound pocket books. Such *aides memoires* have survived as witnesses to the research he undertook for his three major historical fictions, *Esmond*, *The Virginians* and *Denis Duval*. The notebook for *Duval* is the fullest of the three and may well reflect Thackeray's determination to direct his creative energies entirely to history in his later years with the long-meditated 'History of Queen Anne's Reign'. He had, anyway, always been an enthusiastic amateur of the period and over a quarter of the books in his library at the time of his death were printed in the eighteenth century.

The kind of note he kept in his pocket books may be gathered from the transcripts given below of the first and third page of the notebook for *Esmond* (the original is reproduced as pl. 10). The *Esmond* notebook, which is held in the New York Public Library, runs to five pages. As was common with Thackeray the later entries tend to become increasingly scrappy (a deterioration is evident in a comparison of the two examples here). The *Esmond* notebook seems, in fact, to have been used solely for the first third of the novel. Practically the last entry is a trial draft of the opening paragraph of the fifth chapter of the second book which describes the hero's departure for Vigo. It is very likely from this and other entries that

Thackeray gave up keeping a notebook at about the time of writing the Vigo episode. It was at this stage that the novelist obtained the services of an amanuensis, Eyre Crowe, who probably undertook any later research the work required.

Both the following pages reveal Thackeray's appetite for curious period detail, whether social, political, commercial, sartorial, military, topographical or literary. Nonetheless one can see a certain plot-relevance in a number of the entries. From the first Thackeray seems to have been fascinated by Marlborough's duplicity and a proportionately large amount of space is given to references to the treachery at Brest. It is also worth observing that although the notebook was made up during the composition of the early part of the novel characters appear who are to figure prominently later; notably Marlborough but also the Earl of Arran (later Duke Hamilton), Webb and Mohun.

Thackeray did not prepare his notebook for the eyes of readers other than himself. But with a little detective work we can trace much of his preparatory reading. On the first page here the most quoted source is Edward Chamberlayne's *Angliae Notitia Or the Present State of England*. This provides seven of the first fourteen entries. *Angliae Notitia* was a popular and much reprinted compendium which gave an anatomy of court, social and parliamentary life in England. It clearly helped Thackeray construct the historical framework for the opening sections of his novel. That he should have chosen to use 'The One and Twentieth Edition' (London, 1704) indicates his intention to centre the action of his novel in Queen Anne's reign.

Other sources which can be dredged up from page one of the notebook are James Macpherson's *Original Papers, containing the Secret History of Great Britain from the Restoration to the Accession of the House of Hanover*, Dalrymple's *Memoirs of*

Great Britain and Ireland, Henry Sidney's *Diary of the Times of Charles the Second.* These three sources furnished Thackeray with material about the age generally and, more particularly, some of the 'secret history', as Macpherson calls it. Thackeray was always fascinated by what went on behind the historical scenes. Why, he wonders, did Marlborough *really* leave England in 1712? The conviction that great men are not what they publicly seem runs right the way through *Esmond* from the opening chapter with its defence of 'familiar' against 'heroic' history.

Some of the notes on the first page can be seen to resurface in the narrative of the novel. Thackeray is indebted to Chamberlayne for the information about the two prisons where Esmond is held and for the description of his journey along the river after his release. The Duke of Berwick's visit to England is brought into chapter 11. The list of divines which ends the page appears in an early description of Rachel's piety (details can be found in the footnotes).

The second page is sketchier and Thackeray's sources correspondingly harder to come by. Nonetheless we can detect some interesting connections with the novel. The military action which occupies the second book is prefigured in the drawings of the horseman, musketeer and pikeman. From the specific references given it appears that Thackeray was at this stage reading late seventeenth- and early eighteenth-century newspapers, probably for what he called 'gazetteering' (that is chronicling military campaigns). Since we know that he worked in the British Museum it is almost certain that he used the Burney collection of journals and periodicals which the Museum holds. Bound together in the volume for 1698 are *The Postboy, The English Lucian* and *The London Gazette* (two of which Thackeray cites directly). The *Gazette* contains a record of military and naval engagements, *The Postboy* covers the same ground with the addition of a quantity of domestic news and gossip. The *English Lucian* was a comic, somewhat indecent paper of the period. Thackeray could find occasional light relief, however, even in the stodgy pages of *The Postboy*. In the issue for February 24 the news which he notes about the 'paistry cook' runs thus:

Paris, Feb. 24th. Some days since a certain Paistry-Cook was seized by the Lieutenant Generals at *Seve*, which is on the Road to *Versailles*, where he lodged as a Passenger, being accused of Cutting the throats of above 60 Persons, among whom were some Children of Note in this City.

These two pages may be taken as representative of most others and of the way in which the entries in the notebooks become progressively less carefully made. As I have argued in earlier chapters, I feel we may learn something important from this evidence. Despite its apparent miscellaneousness we can see in the notebooks an omnivorous delight in anything connected, however incidentally, with the period in which his fiction was set. And this it is that creates the superbly intimate knowledgeability of the three great historical novels he wrote.

PAGE ONE OF THE ESMOND NOTEBOOK

Kaempfers History of | EUROPE | Japan.[1]
Statue of the Kg. in *Stocks Market*. The neatly wrought Conduit in the Market Place: at the West End of Lombard St., whereupon is placed a very magnificent Statue of K.C.II on Horseback trampling upon an enemy all in white marble at the sole cost of that worthy Citizen and | BARONET | ⟨Alderman⟩ Sir R Viner Knt and Bt.[2]
In King's Square—Soe. Hoe Fields Buildings is another statue of the King very fine.[3]
|*Fleet Brook*. The mighty chargeable and beautiful work rendering

navigable the Fleet Brook a Ditch from the river Thames up to Holborn Bridge; the curious stone bridge over it, the many huge vaults on each side thereof to treasure up Newcastle coals for the use of the poor.[4]

/*Exchanges*. There be many exchanges in London besides Markets and the Royal Exchange—as that stately building called the New Exchange and Exeter Change both in the Strand ⟨where all attire for ladies and gentlemen is sold⟩—not to speak of the Cloysters of Saint Bartholomew and others.[5]

/Golding Square.[6]

/Ralph E of Montague.

The Keeper of the Wardrobe had his office by patent for life, and a salary of 2000.[7]

/Prisons were Newgate Ludgate Q Bench. Fleet. Marshalsea. New Prison White Chappel and Gate House ⟨Westmin⟩.[8]

/Keeping a Christmas. Chamberlayn (1704) 413. a curious account of the manners of the Temple Students.[9]

/In 1694 Churchill sent an express letter to K. James warning him of K. William's design to attack Brest. In Macph. 1.487. 1.456. 499.500.[10]

Lord Arran Son in law of Sunderland and S[11] also in the plot.

I was told by Principal Gordon of the Scots College at Paris that during the hostilities between the D of Marlborough and Ld. Oxford, near the end of the Q's reign, Ld. Oxford who had intelligence of the D's letter and pretended at that time to be in the interests of that family applied for and got a⟨n⟩ |COPY| ⟨order for⟩ the original and that his making the D know that his life was in his hands was the reason of the D's going into a voluntary exile to Brusssells in the year 1712. VII Dalrymple. 1694.[12]

The Duke of Berwick was in England in 1695.[13]

Dr. Tillotson Dr. Patrick D of Peterborow Dr. Stillingfleet D of St. Pauls Dr Jamison Minister of St. Martins. Dr. Sherlock Master of the Temple. Mr. Wake is the wonderfullest young man in the world and the most popular divine now in England.[14] Burnet to Wm.[15]

PAGE THREE OF THE ESMOND NOTEBOOK

[For the three sketches on this page see pl. 10.]

Three ranks fired and 4th. rank of pikemen. They wore their wigs
in bags and all have swords.[16]
As drinkable [?] as
Plumbroth at Xmas and Sillabub in May.[17]
A horse cost 7/– a week at livery. English Lucian March ⟨28⟩
1798.[18]
Lord Mohuns troop of horse in the E of Macclesfields regiment.[19]
Count Tallards palace in St. James's Sq.[20]
A paistry cook at Sêve. this story dates 1698—Postboy Feb 24.[21]

Bibliography

PUBLISHED WORKS BY THACKERAY

1 *Collected Editions*

The Oxford Thackeray, ed. G. Saintsbury, 17 vols, Oxford, 1908.
The Works of William Makepeace Thackeray (the Centenary Biographical edition), with introductions by A. T. Ritchie, 26 vols, London, 1910–1911.

2 *Individual Works*

The History of Henry Esmond, eds J. Sutherland and M. Greenfield, London (Penguin English Library), 1970.
The History of Henry Esmond, ed. W. Allen, New York (Signet Books), 1964.
Vanity Fair, eds G. and K. Tillotson, London, 1963.
Vanity Fair, ed. J. I. M. Stewart, London (Penguin English Library), 1968.

3 *Letters*

The Letters and Private Papers of William Makepeace Thackeray, ed. G. N. Ray, 4 vols, London, 1945–6.
Thackeray's Letters to an American Family, with an introduction by L. W. Baxter, London, 1904.

MANUSCRIPT SOURCES

1 *Manuscripts of Novels*

Denis Duval. Most that Thackeray wrote of this incomplete last novel, up to chapter 7, is housed in the Pierpont Morgan Library. It is entirely autograph.
The History of Henry Esmond. The bulk of this MS. is in the Library of Trinity College Cambridge, though some odd sheets have found their way, via souvenir collections, into other major libraries. The MS. is largely autograph with substantial sections of the second and third

books dictated to Eyre Crowe. Anne Thackeray also took down some of the novel to her father's dictation.

The Newcomes. A large part of the MS. of this novel is held in the library of Charterhouse School. Although well over half of the Charterhouse MS. is in Thackeray's hand he used his daughters extensively as secretaries in the writing of this novel. A sizeable portion of the description of Colonel Newcome's financial ruin is held in the Berg Collection of the New York Public Library; much of it is dictated to a secretary whose hand I cannot identify but who is named in the Library Catalogue as Charles Pearman.

Pendennis. Only chapter 41 and a part of chapter 39 of this novel seem to have survived. Both are in Thackeray's hand and are kept in the College Library at Harvard.

Vanity Fair. The opening section of this novel, up to p. 126 of the Tillotsons' edition, exists in MS. and is held at the Pierpont Morgan Library. It is entirely autograph.

The Virginians. About three-quarters of this novel survives in MS. and is held in the Pierpont Morgan Library, although single sheets and short sections may be found in other major libraries. Thackeray made quite extensive use of secretaries in the writing of this novel only one of whom, Anne Thackeray, I can identify.

2   *Manuscript Working Materials*

Denis Duval. A collection of Thackeray's working materials for this novel is held, together with the novel's MS. in the Pierpont Morgan Library. These papers contain drafts of passages which Thackeray later decided to omit or alter and some forward plans.

Denis Duval. A notebook Thackeray made while preparing this novel and while writing it is held in the Manuscripts Department of the British Museum. It contains memoranda from reading or personal observation and a sketchy master-plan of the narrative.

The History of Henry Esmond. A notebook Thackeray kept while writing *Esmond* is held in the Manuscripts Division of the New York Public Library. It contains period details and sketches and one trial passage of narrative.

The Newcomes. A number-plan for the second half of the novel is owned by Mr R. Taylor and held in the University Library at Princeton.

Philip. A page of proof from the end of the seventeenth chapter with Thackeray's corrections is held in the Pierpont Morgan Library.

BIBLIOGRAPHY

Vanity Fair. A fragmentary plan for the Waterloo chapters is owned by Mr R. Taylor and held in the University Library at Princeton.

The Virginians. A notebook containing observations from Thackeray's reading for the *Four Georges* and the *Virginians* is held in the Beinecke Rare Books Library at Yale.

3 Manuscripts of Works other than Fiction

FROM THE FOUR GEORGES:

GEORGE THE FIRST. The manuscript of this lecture is held in the Pierpont Morgan Library; as was common at this stage of his writing career Thackeray used secretarial assistance. G. Hodder in his *Memories of my Time* gives an account of working with Thackeray on the *Four Georges.*

GEORGE THE THIRD. The manuscript of this lecture is held in the College Library at Harvard.

THACKERAY'S GERMAN SCRAPBOOK. This scrapbook which contains a number of exercise-pieces in prose and verse was made up by the young Thackeray on his visit to Germany in 1830; it is held in the Pierpont Morgan Library.

NOTES FOR A SPEECH. The notes for this speech on Administrative Reform presumably given in 1857 are held in the Pierpont Morgan Library.

4 Sketching Materials

Vanity Fair. Two sheets of sketches Thackeray made for the Waterloo chapters are owned by Mr R. Taylor and are held in the University Library at Princeton.

5 Unpublished Letters

From Thackeray to Mrs J. Blackwood (dated 14 December 1856, held in the Pierpont Morgan Library).

From Thackeray to W. C. Macready (dated 17 February, presumably 1858, owned by Mr R. Taylor and kept in the University Library at Princeton).

From Thackeray to W. F. Synge (dated December 1858, held in the Pierpont Morgan Library).

From Leslie Stephen to the Librarian of Trinity College Cambridge (dated 11 June 1889, held by the College Library).

From Leslie Stephen to T. R. Sullivan (dated 29 September 1893, held in the College Library at Harvard).

Notes

INTRODUCTION

1 James Hannay, *A Brief Memoir* (London, 1864), pp. 20–1.
2 *George Eliot's Life,* ed. J. W. Cross (London and Edinburgh, 1887), p. 441.
3 G. N. Ray, *The Buried Life* (London, 1952), p. 97. See also *Letters and Private Papers of William Makepeace Thackeray,* ed. G. N. Ray (London, 1945), iv, 435.
4 *The Brontës: Their Lives, Friendships and Correspondence,* ed. T. J. Wise and J. A. Symington (Oxford, 1932), iii, 233.
5 'In Memoriam,' *Cornhill Magazine,* ix (Feb. 1864), 130.
6 Eyre Crowe, *Thackeray's Haunts and Homes* (London, 1897), p. 50.
7 A. A. Jack, *Thackeray: A Study* (London, 1895), p. 101.
8 J. T. Fields, *Yesterdays with Authors* (London, 1872), p. 23.
9 C. Whibley, *William Makepeace Thackeray* (London, 1903), p. 246.
10 This and subsequent page references are to the Pocket Edition of Trollope's *Thackeray* (London, 1909).
11 He made the same points in chapter 13 of *An Autobiography* (1883) where, however, he restricted his comments about idleness to Thackeray's later novels.
12 *Notes and Queries,* 252 (26 Aug. 1854), 168.
13 Page (and where necessary volume) references are to the seventeen volume 'Oxford Thackeray' (London, 1908) edited and with introductions by George Saintsbury.
14 See also the notes to the end of his introductions to *Vanity Fair, Pendennis, The Newcomes, The Virginians* and *Philip.*
15 Details of these and other similar lapses may be found in the notes to my Penguin English Library edition of *Esmond* (London, 1970).
16 *Letters,* ii, 346.
17 I have examined some in detail in 'Thackeray's Patchwork: A Note on the Composition of the Eleventh Chapter of *Henry Esmond*', *The Yearbook of English Studies,* I (1971), 141–8. In this one chapter Thackeray changes the season from summer to winter, takes four years off Esmond's life and reverses the order of certain important events in the plot. The most famous of his lapses, however, is that in chapter 59 of *Vanity Fair.* For details see G. N. Ray, *Thackeray: The Uses of Adversity* (London, 1955), pp. 495–6.

18 In various forms the charges are ubiquitous enough in critical writing on Thackeray, but these particular objections may be found in J. Y. T. Greig, *Thackeray: A Reconsideration* (Oxford, 1950), p. 6 and Walter Allen, *The English Novel* (London, 1958), pp. 174–80.

19 From James's review of *Middlemarch* reprinted in *A Century of George Eliot Criticism,* ed. G. S. Haight (London, 1966), p. 81.

20 See M. Elwin, *Thackeray: A Personality* (London, 1932), p. 255.

21 *The Correspondence of J. L. Motley,* ed. G. W. Curtis (London, 1889), i, 279.

22 The letter is dated '29.9.93' and addressed to Thomas Russell Sullivan; it is held in the College Library at Harvard and has never, as far as I know, been printed.

VANITY FAIR: THE ART OF IMPROVISATION

1 See, for example, G. N. Ray, '*Vanity Fair:* One Version of the Novelist's Responsibility', *Essays by Divers Hands,* xxv (1950), 87–101 and the Introduction to *Vanity Fair,* ed. G. and K. Tillotson (London, 1963). Some 110 pages of the manuscript survive and they are mainly interesting for the revisions Thackeray made between first starting work in early 1845 and starting to publish it in early 1847.

2 The illustration is reproduced from the manuscript which is in the Pierpont Morgan Library New York. By this stage in the novel (chapter 13) Thackeray was confidently into his stride and is using his later 'upright' handwriting. A full description of the manuscript can be found in the Tillotsons' edition, pp. 669–80 and it is from this edition that the following printed text and subsequent quotations from the novel are taken.

3 Issued as volume 35 of the Penguin English Library.

4 Mr Robert Taylor's magnificent collection of Thackerayana is held in the Library at Princeton University. All the following items are collected in scrap books of miscellanea, which probably explains why they have been hitherto overlooked.

5 I am grateful to Professor Kathleen Tillotson for pointing out a serious error in my reading of these two scraps.

6 This notebook is held in the Manuscript Division of the British Museum. Its contents are described in the Biographical Introduction to Lady Ritchie's Centenary Biographical Edition of *Denis Duval* and the notes to the unfinished novel. Thackeray makes the following calculation because after years of writing monthly numbers of 32 pages he was unused to preparing novels for the magazine serialization which was intended for *Duval.* Compare with Dickens' memorandum to himself when he turned to magazine serialization with *Hard Times:*

One sheet (16 pages of Bleak House) will make 10 pages and a quarter of Household Words. Fifteen pages of my writing, will make a sheet of Bleak House.

A page and a half of my writing, will make a page of Household Words.

The Quantity of the story to be published weekly, being about five pages of Household Words, will require about *seven pages and a half of my writing.*

See J. Butt and K. Tillotson, *Dickens at Work* (London, 1968), p. 202.

7 See, for example, the praise of J. W. Dodds in his *Thackeray: A Critical Portrait* (Oxford, 1941), p. 113: 'Those critics who complain that Thackeray misses the chance to capitalize on the Duchess of Richmond's ball and the affair at Quatre-Bras are blind to the delicacy of an art which gives him superbly the effect he wanted, and exactly the right effect.'

8 See p. 279 where Osborne shouts to Dobbin: 'Hullo, Dob! Come and drink, old Dob!'

9 See the Tillotsons' *Vanity Fair*, pp. 669–71. Generally speaking the MS. in the sloping hand corresponds to the earliest layer of composition. There is some controversy on the subject of the date of composition of this section. My reasons for disagreeing with the date put forward by the Tillotsons (late 1844) are argued at length in *English Studies*, 53 (Feb. 1972), 47–52.

10 See *Vanity Fair*, p. xviii.

11 Ray, *Thackeray: The Uses of Adversity*, p. 386.

12 The phrase, and the intricate biographical account which supports it, are to be found in Ray's essay '*Vanity Fair:* One Version of the Novelist's Responsibility'.

13 *Letters*, ii, 282.

14 There are two short apostrophes, on p. 83 from 'O, Vanity Fair' to '. . . this season' and on p. 86 from 'Vanity Fair' to '. . . spotless virtue.' The major apostrophe, which is dealt with here, is the passage comprising six paragraphs tagged on to the end of chapter 8.

15 See '*Vanity Fair:* One Version of the Novelist's Responsibility', p. 93.

16 Homer, *Iliad*, vi, 146: 'Men in their generation are like the leaves of the trees.'

17 *Letters*, ii, 539.

18 See *An Autobiography*, ed. F. Page (London, 1950), pp. 370–1.

19 K. Tillotson, *Novels of the Eighteen-Forties* (Oxford, 1954), p. 246.

20 An account of the interview was published in 'An Hour with Thackeray', *Appleton's Journal*, vii (Sept. 1879), 248–54. In the same conversation Cooke alleges that Thackeray told him that all of *Esmond* was dictated.

21 Lord David Cecil, *Early Victorian Novelists* (London, 1934, reprinted 1964), p. 82. See also the Preface of the reprinted volume, p. 7.

22 Ibid., p. 82.

23 The other outstanding examples are Becky's social career in post-war London and her years of exile on the continent both of which are blurred to make them seem shorter than they historically are.
24 This sentence is still legible under Thackeray's crossing out in the MS. at the Pierpont Morgan Library.
25 In chapter 38.
26 See *Letters*, ii, 294, 306.
27 Ray, *Thackeray: The Uses of Adversity*, p. 408.
28 See chapter 37 where Steyne is shown as being among the company in the first scene at 201 Curzon Street.
29 See Ray, *Thackeray: The Uses of Adversity*, pp. 495–6.

PENDENNIS: THE TWO THACKERAYS AND THE LIMITS OF AUTOBIOGRAPHICAL FICTION

1 *Thackeray's Letters to an American Family*, ed. L. Baxter (London, 1904), p. 6.
2 What little survives of the *Pendennis* manuscript (i.e. most of chapter 41 and part of chapter 39) is held in the College Library at Harvard. For the finally printed version of this passage see pp. 517–18.
3 This poem, and others like it, are preserved in a scrapbook held by the Pierpont Morgan Library.
4 For the printed version see p. 520. Thackeray dealt with many of the issues raised by Pen and Warrington in their 'philosophical conversation' in Yellowplush's *Epistles to the Literati* (Jan. 1840). There clearly speaking for Thackeray, though with his usual idiosyncratic spelling, Yellowplush tells the pretentious literary artist Bulwer Lytton: 'You wrote ... for money, — money from the maniger, money from the bookseller, — for the same reason that I write this. Sir, Shakespeare wrote for the very same reasons, and I never heard that he bragged about serving the drama. Away with this canting about great motifs! Let us not be too proud, my dear Barnet, and fansy ourselves marters of the truth, marters or apostels. We are but tradesmen, working for bread and not for righteousness' sake' (i, 320).
5 For the printed version see p. 521.
6 For the printed version see pp. 521–2.
7 For the printed version see p. 522.
8 At least one critic has commented on this as a fine stroke by Thackeray, though without realising that it was a revision. See J. McMaster, *Thackeray: The Major Novels* (London, 1971), p. 81.
9 For the printed version see pp. 523–4.
10 See Greig, *Thackeray: A Reconsideration*, pp. 126–7.
11 Charlotte Brontë realised the element of autobiography in Warrington.

See, for example, Lionel Stevenson, *The Showman of Vanity Fair* (London, 1947), p. 236. Stevenson, who in many ways gives the best account of the Thackeray–Brontë relationship, quotes the following anecdote on how Charlotte Brontë responded on being introduced by the other novelist as 'Jane Eyre':

> '. . . what would you have thought of me if I had introduced you to my father, before a mixed company of strangers, as "Mr. Warrington"?'
> Thackeray replied, 'No, you mean "Arthur Pendennis".'
> 'No, I *don't* mean Arthur Pendennis!' retorted Miss Brontë; 'I mean Mr. Warrington, and Mr. Warrington would not have behaved as you behaved to me yesterday.'

12 Fraser's Magazine, 43, January 1851.
13 See, for example, the opening pages of *The Virginians*. Anonymous editors are present in *Pendennis* and *The Virginians*, family editors in *Esmond* and Arthur Pendennis himself edits the *Newcomes* and *Philip*. *Denis Duval* was originally to have had an editor (see chapter 6 of this study) but Thackeray removed him, presumably so as to get a faster movement in his narrative.
14 Geoffrey Tillotson, *Thackeray the Novelist* (Cambridge, 1954), p. 62.

HENRY ESMOND
AND THE VIRTUES OF CARELESSNESS

1 G. N. Ray, *Thackeray: The Age of Wisdom* (London, 1958), p. 176.
2 *Leader*, 6 November 1852, reprinted in *Thackeray: The Critical Heritage*, ed. G. Tillotson and D. Hawes (London, 1968), p. 137.
3 Part of this correspondence is quoted in the introduction to the Oxford edition, p. xxvii. Stephen's letters are with the manuscript in the possession of Trinity College, Cambridge. A description of the MS. may be found in the page quoted above in the Oxford edition and in the Preface to the Penguin English Library edition of the novel, pp. 29–30.
4 Eyre Crowe, *With Thackeray in America* (London, 1893), p. 3.
5 Elwin, *Thackeray*, pp. 272–3.
6 Greig, *Thackeray: A Reconsideration*, p. 160.
7 See Ray, *The Buried Life*, p. 97.
8 This element in the story is examined authoritatively by J. E. Tilford's 'The "Unsavoury Plot" of *Henry Esmond*', *Nineteenth Century Fiction*, 6 (Sept. 1951), 121–30.
9 *The George Eliot Letters*, ed. G. S. Haight (New Haven, Conn., 1955), ii, 67.
10 J. E. Tilford in 'The Love Theme of *Henry Esmond*', *PMLA*, 67 (1952), 684–701, makes a strong case for the preconceived unity of *Esmond*.

11 'The whole race of living creatures.' Thackeray took this quotation from Fielding's *Tom Jones*, book 5, chapter 11, second paragraph.

12 For details see the previously cited article 'Thackeray's Patchwork', in the *Yearbook of English Studies*, 1971.

13 *Letters*, ii, 807.

14 See the Penguin English Library edition of *Esmond*, p. 518.

15 This assertion may be found in the *Dictionary of National Biography* entry on Thackeray, lx, 103.

16 *Letters*, iii, 446–8.

17 T. B. Macaulay, *The History of England* (London, 1885), iv, 512.

18 For the subsequent attack on Macaulay over his Marlborough material, see John Paget's *New Examen* (London, 1860).

THE NEWCOMES: THE WELL PLANNED BAGGY MONSTER

1 The fragment of the plan is in the Taylor collection at Princeton University. It is reprinted, with perceptive commentary, in Ray's *Thackeray: The Age of Wisdom*, p. 469.

2 Ibid., p. 469.

3 Ray, *The Buried Life*, p. 113.

4 Canon J. W. Irvine, 'A Study for Colonel Newcome', *Nineteenth Century*, xxxiv, Oct. 1893, 589. Irvine dates the visit as the third or fourth of April 1855.

5 Originally to be found in the Preface to James's *The Tragic Muse*.

6 *Letters*, iii, 675. There is a stark nobility in the diaries of the later years which, for the most part contain only the record of social engagements, bouts of illness and spells of work.

7 I would guess that Thackeray fell into this method of planning from the years of experience in devising two episodes for illustration each month.

8 Quoted in Lady Ritchie's introduction to *The Newcomes*, Centenary Biographical Edition (London, 1912), pp. xlvii–viii.

9 *Letters of James Russell Lowell*, ed. C. E. Norton (New York, 1894), i, 239.

10 Greig, *Thackeray: A Reconsideration*, p. 178.

11 Kathleen Tillotson, *Novels of the Eighteen-Forties* (Oxford, 1954), pp. 47–53.

12 This encounter is recorded in an article on James Russell Lowell in *Harper's New Monthly Magazine*, Vol. 62 (Jan. 1881), 265–6.

13 See J. A. Sutherland, 'The Inhibiting Secretary in Thackeray's Fiction,' *Modern Language Quarterly*, No. 2, Vol. 32 (June 1971), 175–88. This article also gives a description of the surviving MS. of *The Newcomes* at Charterhouse School, from which the following text of Newcome's death is taken.

14 Introduction to *The Newcomes*, Centenary Biographical Edition, p. li.
15 In the printed text the Christian name of Madame de Florac is 'Léonore'. In the first edition there is some inconsistency on this point, but I would guess 'Léonore' was finally preferred for its allusion to the heroine of Bürger's famous ballad who was separated from her lover and, herself still living, reunited with him after his death.
16 For the printed version of this scene see pp. 1006–7 of the Oxford edition. This edition also offers a facsimile of part of the autograph manuscript description of Colonel Newcome's death in its introduction.
17 Thackeray's preoccupation with 'spiritual' sexuality was, I believe, first discussed by Walter Allen in his afterword to his Signet edition of *Henry Esmond* (New York, 1964), pp. 465–77.

THE VIRGINIANS: THE WORST NOVEL ANYONE EVER WROTE

1 Douglas Jerrold is popularly supposed to have replied when Thackeray confessed that *The Virginians* was the worst novel he ever wrote: 'No. It's the worst novel anyone ever wrote.' Elwin points out in his *Thackeray: A Personality* (p. 244) that the exchange was impossible since Jerrold died in 1857, before the novel was finished.
2 A notebook in which Thackeray stored his historical research for *The Virginians* has survived and is held at the Beinecke Library, Yale. Pages 9 and 10 deal with the execution of Scottish Rebels in the '45 uprising. This suggests Thackeray may have toyed with the idea of a revolutionary setting nearer home for his novel. On the other hand many of the early entries in the notebook (up to page 11 of its 24 pages, in fact) seem to prepare for the lectures on the *Four Georges*—so it is possible that Thackeray was merely scrap-hunting for interesting historical miscellanea in his reading in the period.
3 'Preserving' is, of course, Macaulay's famous epithet for the English Revolution of 1688. The link with North America is suggested in the first and second paragraphs of the first chapter of the *History of England*.
4 J. H. Stonehouse's *Catalogue of the Libraries of Charles Dickens and W. M. Thackeray* (London, 1935) is instructive in this respect. In comparison with the other novelist Thackeray's collection of books is remarkable for the number of scholarly historical works it contains.
5 See J. R. Harvey, *Victorian Novelists and their Illustrators* (London, 1970), pp. 98–9.
6 'A Glimpse of Thackeray', *Hours at Home*, x (March 1870), 402–5. My reference is taken from Ray, *Thackeray: The Age of Wisdom*, p. 382.
7 *Letters*, iii, 216.
8 *Letters*, iv, 108–9.

9 These fragmentary notes are printed on p. xxxiv of Lady Ritchie's Biographical Introduction to her Centenary Biographical Edition of *The
Virginians* (Vol. XVI of the series). I have been unable to locate the particular notebook from which she quotes.

10 *Letters*, iv, 115.

11 *Letters*, iv, 135.

12 Whitwell Elwin (ed. Warwick Elwin), *Some XVIII Century Men of
Letters* (London, 1902), i, 187.

13 Like most of Thackeray's literary remains the MS. of *The Virginians* has
been dispersed fairly widely on both sides of the Atlantic. But most of it is
held in the Pierpont Morgan Library, and it is to the MS. there that I refer.
There is no description of the MS. in print. In general it conforms to the
pattern of Thackeray's later mode of working: short spells of composition,
neater handwriting than in his earlier career, frequent reliance on the assistance of secretaries to take down dictation, and considerable chopping and
sandwiching of stretches of narrative, especially towards the end of the
novel.

14 Elwin, *Some XVIII Century Men of Letters.*

15 See J. Lester, 'Thackeray's Narrative Technique', *PMLA*, 69, 1954,
392–409, for an excellent analysis of Thackeray's habit of 'redoubling' in
his narrative.

16 See *An Autobiography*, ed. F. Page (Oxford, 1950), p. 144.

17 *George Gissing's Commonplace Book*, ed. J. Korg (New York, 1962), p.
30.

18 *Harper's New Monthly Magazine* (New York), 92, Jan. 1858, 270. Early
impressions of the novel were sold to the American Magazine 'for which'
an advertisement said on the back cover, 'the Publishers pay Mr. Thackeray
the sum of Two Thousand Dollars'. *Harper's* began serialising the novel
in their December 1857 issue.

19 Ray, *Thackeray: The Age of Wisdom*, p. 426.

20 *An Autobiography*, ed. F. Page (Oxford, 1950), p. 244.

21 See the 'Editor's Easy Chair' in *Harper's*, 92, Jan. 1858, 270: 97, June 1858,
123: 103, Dec. 1858, 126.

22 *The Letters of George Meredith*, ed. C. L. Cline (Oxford, 1970), i, 32.

23 Ibid., i, 41.

24 See Ray, *Thackeray: The Age of Wisdom*, p. 235.

25 Since he gave his lectures on the Georges in many places over a period of
years the MSS. tend to be composite with many afterthought revisions and
rewritten passages. Nonetheless what I quote above seems to be version
of the lecture given in America. The MS. is in the Pierpont Morgan
Library. The excised passage would have come on p. 711 of the Oxford
edition text, tagged on to the paragraph ending: '. . . and the Residenz'.

26 From the same MS. as above. This extract would have come in the para-

graph beginning 'That was a curious state . . .' on p. 708 of the Oxford edition.

27 The MS. of the George III lecture is held in the College Library, Harvard. The quoted passage would have come on p. 770 of the Oxford edition. It is, in fact, crossed out in the MS. but this is because, I believe, Thackeray, used his corrected reading script to send to the printers.

28 See Vol. XIII of the Oxford edition and pp. xxiii and 693–4.

29 For an account of Thackeray's connection with Administrative Reform see Ray, *Thackeray: The Age of Wisdom*, pp. 250–7. Thackeray made a number of speeches on the subject of Reform which have never been collected or, often, reported. The notes for one survive in his handwriting in the Pierpont Morgan Library. (The person who described the MS. for its sale, wrongly, I think, attributes it in an accompanying note to Thackeray's election campaign at Oxford in July 1857.) A short sample will give an impression of the tone of the whole: '. . . Some gentlemen here have been very angry with Lord Palmerston. I would refer such to the august advice lately delivered by his Royal Highness Prince Albert at the Trinity House—and thence to go forth *urbi et orbi* to the city and the respectful Universe. Deal gently with your Governors said H.R.H.—be to their faults a little blind, be to their virtues very kind. Do not be rude to the old gentlemen. Don't you see what a fix they are in? Administrative Reformers! listen to the counsel of the Princely Peacemaker, and draw your censures mild. I remember once sitting with a friend in the pit of this very theatre where we are now exhibiting our private theatricals. I had come to see a new comedy. I forget what—it was a very dreary new comedy— with jokes almost as mild as that of Lord Palmerston's which has made gentlemen so angry. The hero and young man of fashion of the piece was a certain old actor—whom I have seen on these boards any time these forty years who surely ought to know how to act the part of a fashionable young dog, having performed it so long. When he appeared, in the midst of the drear silence which generally pervaded the performance, my friend called out—By Jove! How stale Popjoy is!—And he spoke in a perfectly audible voice, and the audience laughed at that, more, I think, than at any joke in the piece. The Downing Street Popjoys are rather stale. Called to the government as he undoubtedly was by the national acclamation the Manager of the St. Stephens Theatre has made up his company with such a set of old bigwigs, Old Whigs from Brooks's . . .'

30 An extract from Edmund Yates's attack on Thackeray in his *Town Talk* of June 1858; see *Letters*, iv, 89–106.

31 The letter, which is in the Pierpont Morgan Library, is dated 14 Dec. 1856. It has never been printed, as far as I know.

32 *Harper's*, 92, Jan. 1858, 271.

33 This deleted passage would have come on p. 68 of the Oxford edition text.

34 *Harper's*, 94, March 1858, 558. The letter is signed 'Newark' and dated Feb. 1858. The controversy about Thackeray's depiction of Washington was still simmering in the magazine in mid-summer (see *Harper's*, 98 July 1858, 269).

35 Quoted in Lady Ritchie's Biographical Introduction to the Centenary Biographical edition of *The Virginians*, vol. xvi, p. xxxi.

36 This is evident from its being on Athenaeum Club notepaper, whereas the chapter in which it is set is on uncrested paper.

37 The assertion is best set in the Centenary Biographical edition of *The Virginians*, xvii, 101, where it is accompanied by an appropriate Thackerayan vignette.

38 The letter is to W. F. Synge and is dated Dec. 1858. It is in the Pierpont Morgan Library and has never been printed, as far as I know.

DENIS DUVAL: THE SERIALIST AND THE SCHOLAR

1 *The Newcomes*, xiv, 296.

2 See the 'Notes' appended by F. Greenwood (originally in *The Cornhill* in June 1864) to the unfinished narrative of *Duval*, reprinted in the Oxford edition, xvii, 332–45 and the Centenary Biographical edition, xxi, 140–55. See also Ray, *Thackeray: The Age of Wisdom*, 409–10.

3 Seven chapters set up in proof, with Thackeray's corrections, are in the Manuscript Division of the British Museum. With them is a notebook, referred to later in this chapter, which contains some eighteen pages of notes for the novel, particularly its historical background. The manuscript of the incomplete *Duval* is in the Pierpont Morgan Library. It is described, and a page of it reproduced, in the Biographical Introduction to Lady Ritchie's Centenary Biographical edition (Vol. xxi). Lady Ritchie also reproduces a page of the notebook in the same Introduction.

4 *An Autobiography*, ed. F. Page (Oxford, 1950), pp. 256–7.

5 *The House of Smith Elder*, Printed for Private Circulation (London, 1923), p. 70.

6 Thackeray regularly tried to get a few numbers ahead in his writing, and as regularly failed. See, for example, a letter to his mother while writing *Pendennis* in July 1849: 'I woonder [*sic*] could I do 2 [Numbers] next month? . . . but thats [*sic*] too great a piece of luck to hope for: the invention seems to fail for one number almost how much more for 2' (see *Letters*, ii, 568).

7 This and similar lamentations about being an 'extinct volcano' were made frequently by Thackeray in his later years. See for example his relative F. St John Thackeray's 'Reminiscences of William Makepeace Thackeray' in *Temple Bar*, July 1893 and Ray's *Thackeray: The Age of Wisdom*, pp. 322–70.

8 The letter, dated May 23, 1858, is printed in *John Blackwood*, By his Daughter Mrs Gerald Porter (Edinburgh, 1898), p. 42.

9 *The Correspondence of J. L. Motley*, ed. G. W. Curtis (London, 1889), i, 279–80.

10 This letter has not, I believe, been printed. It is in the possession of Mr Robert Taylor. It is addressed to William Charles Macready and dated '17 February' (presumably 1858).

11 *Letters* ii, 519.

12 See pp. 257, 281–2.

13 Ioan Williams, *Thackeray* (London, 1968), p. 79.

14 *Letters*, iv, 425.

15 *Fraser's Magazine*, 43, Jan. 1851, 86.

16 Taken from the notebook for *Duval* in the British Museum. Greenwood prints a version of this sketch in his notes to the unfinished novel, see also *Letters*, iv, 292–3. The business about the Westons' trial is taken *verbatim* from the *Annual Register* for 1782, p. 214.

17 See Appendix 1 for other aspects of Thackeray's long distance planning.

18 See Note 31 to this chapter.

19 The notebook for *Esmond* is in the Manuscript Division of the New York Public Library. Its contents are along the same lines as those notebooks Thackeray kept while preparing for *Duval* and *The Virginians*, though it is somewhat shorter (five pages). The illustrated extract from the notebook and that quoted later in the chapter may be taken as typical.

20 This was the abortive *Knights of Borsellen*, a project which Thackeray had long meditated. See Ray, *Thackeray: The Age of Wisdom*, p. 408.

21 J. C. Hotten (i.e. 'Theodore Taylor'), *Thackeray: The Humourist and the Man of Letters* (London, 1864), p. 186.

22 See Lady Ritchie's Biographical Introduction to the Centenary Biographical edition of *Denis Duval*, p. xii, for Thackeray's desire for 'story' in his last novel. The quotation 'an incident . . . in every chapter' is taken from the Oxford edition of the *Roundabout Papers*, xvii, 596. It is interesting that the notebook for *Duval* shows that the first reading Thackeray did for the novel was in the *Gentleman's Magazine* and its accounts of the trials of recent criminals (among whom were La Motte and the Westons).

23 Lester Wallack, *Memories of Fifty Years* (New York, 1889), p. 206.

24 G. Hodder, *Memories of my Time* (London, 1870), p. 252.

25 *Letters*, iv, 436.

26 Together with the MS. of *Duval* at the Morgan Library are some end-papers. Two pages, numbered 5–6 are among them and from them the quotations are taken. Thackeray was frugal with his writing paper and the opening of chapter 2 in the MS. begins with a crossed out passage which is continuous with the above pages 5 and 6 (also crossed out at the top of the sheet is the page number '7'). This is obviously a relic of some windy,

experimental first chapter; it contains for example the passage which was later adapted for the novel's first paragraph in its final form: '| MR. DUVAL WAS NO HIGHWAYMAN'S GRANDSON, BUT A DESCENDANT OF ONE OF MANY FRENCH PROTESTANT FAMILIES WHO SETTLED IN ENGLAND AFTER THEIR EXPULSION FROM THEIR NATIVE COUNTRY |'.

27 See the Centenary Biographical edition of *Duval*, pp. xxix–xxxi. It will be noted that this unpublished first chapter is written in the person of a biographer-narrator. The MS. of this chapter is among the end-papers at the Morgan Library. It is fair-written and was obviously intended, at the time of writing, to be a finished draft.

28 P. xxix of the Centenary Biographical edition of *Duval*. Following references are also to this edition.

29 The phrase is taken from the *Roundabout Papers*, written at much the same time as *Duval* and in which Thackeray turns over and again to the theme of time's passing (see 'De Finibus' or 'De Juventute' for example).

30 I must confess that there is an element of hypothesis at this stage of the reconstruction of the novel's composition. This opening is found at the top of what appears to have been an original first page of the MS. What precedes it in the finished text (see the next quotation) does not fill a sheet and seems to have been written for insertion later.

31 MS. letter among the *Duval* end-papers in the Morgan Library. The italics are mine, and the reference to Agincourt alludes to Thackeray's earlier *Knights of Borsellen* project.

32 See the Centenary Biographical edition, p. xiii.

33 This is to be found on a MS. sheet among the endpapers to *Duval*. The reference to Eve and the apple will be found on pp. 19–20 of the Centenary Biographical edition.

34 See p. 14 of *Duval* and p. 26.

35 See p. 141 of the Centenary Biographical edition where Greenwood's notes are conveniently reprinted.

36 Taken from the *Duval* notebook in the British Museum. This entry is typical of many others. The Holloway referred to is William, who wrote a *History of Rye* (London, 1847). Pecock's School is mentioned on p. 402.

37 It is interesting to note that Thackeray's favourite reference books while preparing for his novels were the cyclopaedic and miscellaneous *Annual Register*, *Gentleman's Magazine* and *Biographie Universelle*.

38 *Letters*, ii, 761. Thackeray's comments refer specifically to the lectures on the 'Eighteenth Century Humourists' which he was giving at the time.

39 This sketch is jotted down separately on a sheet of paper preserved among the endpapers to the Duval MS. in the Morgan Library. Thackeray adopted the first part and used it, see pp. 8–9 of the Centenary Biographical edition of the novel. The second item about bringing up the kegs is also found on page 12 of the *Duval* notebook and appears on p. 75 of the novel.

40 See *Letters*, iii, 49, 54, where Thackeray congratulates himself on having seen Blenheim 'in the spirit' while writing *Esmond*.

41 See Lady Ritchie's Biographical Introduction to *Duval*, p. xiv.

42 *Letters*, iv, 293–4.

43 See *Duval*, p. 126.

44 J. Brown, *Thackeray: His Literary Career* (Boston, 1877), pp. 37–8.

45 'In Memoriam', p. 131.

46 *Edinburgh Review*, 87, Jan. 1848, 60.

47 Eyre Crowe, *Thackeray's Haunts and Homes*, pp. 55–6. See also, J. Stevens, 'A Note on Thackeray's Manager of the Performance', *Nineteenth Century Fiction*, 22 (Mar. 1968), 391–7.

48 *Letters*, iv, 292.

49 From the *Duval* Notebook in the British Museum. These notes are to be found on pages 8–9. The Murray referred to is John Murray's *A Handbook for Travellers in Kent and Sussex* (London, 1858).

50 From the *Esmond* Notebook in the New York Public Library.

51 Sir Charles Firth, *A Commentary on Macaulay's History of England* (London, 1938, reprinted 1964), p. 9.

52 Ibid.

53 *Letters*, iii, 38.

54 See Lewis Melville, *William Makepeace Thackeray: A Biography* (London, 1910), ii, 55–6.

APPENDIX ONE: THE LOCAL PLANS FOR *DENIS DUVAL*

1 From an un-numbered sheet among the end-papers to the *Duval* MS. in the Morgan Library. The stretch of composition particularly concerned in this plan will be found on pp. 10–25 of the Centenary Biographical edition of *Duval*.

2 From a sheet among the end-papers to the *Duval* MS. in the Morgan Library.

3 A note on the opposite page of the notebook tells us that this is Hurd's opinion of David Hume.

4 This detail of the invasion panic in June 1779 is taken from the fifth volume of Dr John Campbell's *Lives of the British Admirals* (London, 1813).

APPENDIX TWO: THE *ESMOND* NOTEBOOK

1 Thackeray probably indicates here the first English translation of E. Kaempfer's *History of Japan* (London, 1727) entered in the British Museum Catalogue. Its irrelevance to any event in *Esmond* suggests that

the novelist may have originally intended the notebook for random jottings on various subjects.

2 This description of Charles II's statue is taken from Edward Chamberlayne's *Angliae Notitia Or the Present State of England, The One and Twentieth Edition* (London, 1704), p. 436. Viner (1631–88) was Lord Mayor of London. The statue was taken down in 1736 to make room for the Mansion House, built on the site of the former Stocks Market.

3 An entry in *Angliae Notitia*, p. 436 runs: 'FOUNTAIN IN KINGS SQUARE. The design also of that Fountain in the middle of King's Square in *Soe-Hoe Fields* Buildings, deserves observation; where, on a high pedestal, is King *Charles's* statue . . .' King's Square is now Soho Square.

4 Taken from *Angliae Notitia*, pp. 436–7.

5 Adapted from an entry on p. 437 of *Angliae Notitia*.

6 There is no Golding Square in London as far as I know. There is, however, a Golden Square. In the manuscript of the tenth chapter of the second book Thackeray wrote 'it was in London, in Golding Square, where Major-General Webb lodged . . .' which was changed in the printed version of the text to 'Golden Square' (see p. 242). In the notebook Thackeray was presumably marking down the residence of his illustrious ancestor who is to figure later in the action.

7 These details about the Earl of Montagu are taken from *Angliae Notitia*, pp. 440–1.

8 *Angliae Notitia*, pp. 426–7, lists these London prisons in exactly the same order as Thackeray here. See *Esmond*, p. 163.

9 On *Angliae Notitia*, pp. 412–13, is a description of the mock parliament the students of the Inns of Court elect at Christmas and the festivities which follow.

10 The reference is to James MacPherson, *Original Papers, containing the Secret History of Great Britain from the Restoration to the Accession of the House of Hanover* (London, 1775, 2 vols.). 'i. 487' records Churchill's alleged letter to the 'King of England' (i.e. James II) dated May 1694, informing him of the military details of the proposed Brest raid by the English forces (see *Esmond*, p. 286). 'i. 456' and '499.500' have to do with the intrigues to return James to the throne of England.

11 I.e. 'and Sunderland'. Sunderland's son-in-law became in later life the fourth Duke of Hamilton. In the narrative of *Esmond* he is betrothed to Beatrix and killed in a duel by Mohun (as he was in historical fact). In this entry Thackeray seems to be drawing on a letter quoted in MacPherson's *Original Papers*, i, 475.

12 Quoted from J. Dalrymple, *Memoirs of Great Britain and Ireland* (London, 1788), iii, 45. The letter referred to is Marlborough's, warning James of the Brest expedition.

13 The Duke of Berwick, who was the natural son of James, visited England

clandestinely in 1695. The visit is mentioned by MacPherson (see also the visit by 'Captain James'—i.e. James Fitzjames Duke of Berwick—in *Esmond*, p. 121).

14 This list and the eulogistic comment about Wake is taken from a letter from 'Dr. Burnet to the Prince of Orange' reproduced in Henry Sidney, *Diary of the Times of Charles the Second* (London, 1843), ii, 281–5 (see *Esmond*, p. 100).

15 I.e. Gilbert Burnet to William of Orange.

16 I have not been able to trace this piece of military information.

17 I have not been able to trace this quotation.

18 1798 is here, I take it, a mistake for 1698. There is an issue of *The English Lucian* for March 28 which is found in the Burney collection a few pages on from the *Postboy* quoted later on the page.

19 In 1694 Mohun volunteered for the Brest expedition and was made a captain in Lord Macclesfield's regiment. He served with distinction until 1696. On page 294 of *Esmond* Thackeray mentions Mohun, anachronistically, as still commanding the troop ten years later.

20 See the *Postboy*, Feb. 22, 1698: 'Count *Tallard* is expected here in 10 or 12 days, by which time his Palace in St. James's Square will be fitted up for his Reception.'

21 See the foregoing introduction for the anecdote about the pastry-cook.

Index

163

Gissing, George, 95
Goldsmith, Oliver, 91–2
Greig, J. Y. T., 51, 57, 80, 148

Hannay, J., 1
Harper's Magazine, 97–8, 103–6, 154, 156
Hayward, A., 127
Hodder, G., 118
Hogarth, W., 87
Horace, 11, 115

Iphigenia, 11–17
Irvine, J. W., 152

Jack, A. A., 1–2
Jacob and Rachel, 62
James, Henry, 7, 77, 90, 107
Jephthah, 14
Jerrold, D., 89, 153
Johnson, Dr, 92
Jones, Paul, 137
Jude the Obscure, 107

La Motte, Count de, 110, 115, 116, 122–3, 137
Lester, J., 154
Lewes, G., 56, 112
Lockwood, John, 5–6, 67
Lowell, J. R., 81, 152

Macaulay, T. B., 68, 86–7, 89, 130–132
McMaster, J., 150
MacPherson, J., 71, 128, 139–42
Macready, W. C., 112
Marlborough, Duke of, 68, 70–1, 140–2
Meredith, George, 99, 107

Mohun, H., 64
Motley, J. L., 8, 112

Newcome, Barnes, 74–6
Newcome, Lady Clara, 74–6
Newcome, Clive, 74–5, 79, 83–4
Newcome, Ethel, 74–5, 79, 82–4
Newcome, Colonel Thomas, 74–85
Notes and Queries, 3, 128

O'Dowd, Major and Mrs, 19, 22
Osborne, Mr, 12–17, 36, 39
Osborne, George, 12–17, 23, 38

Pendennis, Arthur, 45–55, 62, 75–6, 85, 113, 119–20
Pendennis, Helen, 52, 61–2, 113
Pendennis, Major, 75, 78, 79, 80
Punch, 29

Raggles, 42–3
Ray, G. N., 24–34 *passim*, 40, 54, 56, 59, 74, 76, 97, 144, 147
Ridley, J. J., 90, 107
Ritchie, Lady A., 57, 79, 81, 144, 154

Saintsbury, G., 4, 98, 101–2, 144
Saverne, Agnes de, 110–11, 120–2, 133–4
Scott, Sir Walter, 62, 117
Sedley, Amelia, 12–17, 19–22, 26, 33, 36–7, 39, 44
Sedley, John, 40
Sedley, Jos, 19–22, 36, 38
Sharp, Becky, 13, 20–1, 25–8, 31–4, 36–8, 41–3
Sievewright, Nancy, 59
Smith, G., 122